Science Alive

Takayuki Ishii   Masahiko Iwata   Joe Ciunci

photographs by
iStockphoto

音声ファイルのダウンロード／ストリーミング

CDマーク表示がある箇所は、音声を弊社HPより無料でダウンロード／ストリーミングすることができます。下記URL の書籍詳細ページに音声ダウンロードアイコンがございますのでそちらから自習用音声としてご活用ください。

https://www.seibido.co.jp/ad709

Science Alive

Copyright © 2025 by Takayuki Ishii, Masahiko Iwata, Joe Ciunci

*All rights reserved for Japan.
No part of this book may be reproduced in any form
without permission from Seibido Co., Ltd.*

はじめに

　科学の発展は、現代の生活文化に大きな影響を与えています。本テキストは、科学分野の英文パッセージを通して、科学の知識と英語力を身に付ける総合テキストです。

　「当たり前のことを掘り下げる」「一般的に言われていることを疑う」「２つのものを比べてみる」「ある分野で一番のものを探す」という４つの視点は、新たな知見を得るのに必要なものと思われます。本書は、このような視点から、英文パッセージを作成しています。

　本テキストの科学のテーマとしては、５つのジャンルを想定しています。それは、「人間」（１章〜３章）、「健康」（４章〜６章）、「テクノロジー」（７章〜９章）、「動物」（10章〜12章）、そして、「物理化学」（13章〜15章）の５つです。

　また、総合的な英語力を培うには、英語力の基本となる語彙力、文法力、更に、４技能、即ち、インプットの力（リスニングやリーディング）とアウトプットの力（スピーキングやライティング）、つまり、トータルで６つの力を、有機的に結び付けて伸ばしていく必要があります。

　本書は、各章について、１頁目を ① Vocabulary Check、２頁目を ② Reading Passage、３頁目を ③ Comprehension、４頁目を ④ Grammar、５頁目を ⑤ Composition、６頁目を ⑥ Listening and Dictation、７頁目を ⑦ Talk and Discussion として構成されています。

　英語の６つの力と上記の①〜⑦の対応については、語彙力は①と②の Notes、文法力は④、リスニングは⑥、スピーキングは⑦、リーディングは②と③、ライティングは⑤と⑥の Dictation によって養えるようテキストが編まれています。

　最後に、コラムとして、(1) 文法コラム（その章のテーマの文法事項を簡単にまとめたもの）、(2) 科学よもやま話（その章のテーマに関する面白情報）、(3)Useful Expressions（トークやディスカッションで使える表現）、および (4) コミュニケーションのコツ（コミュニケーションをとる上でのヒントと考え方）の４つを用意しています。

　本テキストの第１章〜第３章、第10章〜第13章、および、第15章は (但し、担当章の Grammar Points と Talk and Discussion を除く) は岩田が、第４章〜第９章、および、第14章、そして、全章の Grammar Points と Talk and Discussion のページ、更に、全体の監修を石井が、英文校閲全てを Ciunci が担当しました。

　最新の科学に関して、最先端の情報、面白い雑学、奥深い知見、役に立つ知識を英語で学びつつ、英語の６つの力（語彙力、文法力、リーディング、ライティング、リスニング、スピーキング）の涵養に少しでも貢献できれば、本書の著者として、これに勝る喜びはありません。

著者代表　石井　隆之

本書の使い方

各章 7 ページで構成され、全 15 章からなります。各章の構成と使い方を示します。

Vocabulary Check

Reading Passage に出てくる重要な単語の定義を選ぶ問題 7 問。

Reading

Reading Passage は章のタイトルに関するもので、400 語を超えない程度の長さとし、専門的な言葉はあるものの、できるだけ難しくならない表現を用いています。

Notes：特にレベルの高い語句についてその意味を挙げています。

Comprehension

1. 3 つの文が本文の内容と一致しているか、いないかを確認させる問題を 3 問出題。一致していたら T、一致していなければ F を記入する形式です。
2. 質問に対する答えを 4 つの選択肢から選ぶ問題を 3 問出題しています。

Grammar Points

☆コラム 1　英文法のコラム：その章のテーマとなる文法事項を簡単に説明しています。上記のコラムの後に、Reading Passage に出てきた文法項目に関する問題が 5 問。空欄に当てはまる語句を 4 つの中から選ぶ形式。問題文は、原則として、文法項目に関係する文を Reading Passage から抜粋し、少し言い換えた形をとっています。

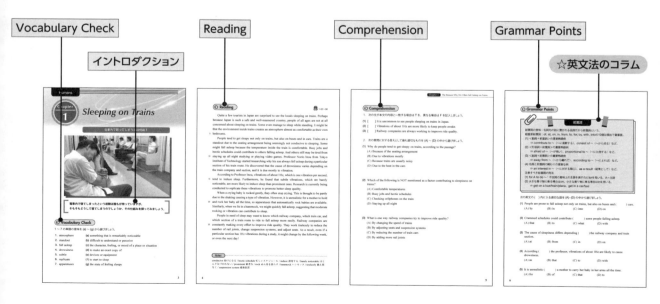

Composition Clues

比較的重要な熟語や構文を用いた、その章のテーマに関する文の一部を並べ替える問題が5問。5つの語(句)を並べ替える形式。5つの語(句)はアルファベット順です。

Listening and Dictation

Reading Passage の要約文（130語前後）を聞いて、ディクテーションを行い、空欄を埋める問題で、空欄は10カ所。その後、空欄に当てはまる単語を下の枠内から選び、記号で答えます。枠内の単語はアルファベット順に並んでいます。

☆コラム2 科学よもやま話：その章のテーマに関する興味深い情報を提供しています。

Talk and Discussion

その章のテーマに関する、または、テーマから発展する事象に関するトピックを2つ挙げて、トークやディスカッションをします。英語を用い、ペアやグループで行うのが基本的な形です。

☆コラム3 Useful Expressions：設定されたトピックに基づき、トークやディスカッションを行うのに役立つ表現を5つ挙げています。空所に必要な表現を入れる形式です。

☆コラム4 コミュニケーションのコツ：英語でのコミュニケーションをとるのに知っておくと便利な情報を挙げています。

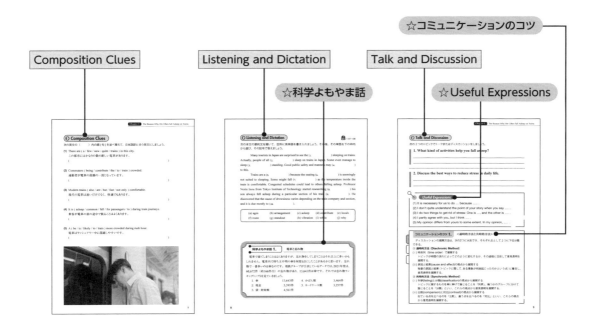

Contents

はじめに iii

本書の使い方 iv

Humans

Chapter 1.. p3

Sleeping on Trains
電車内で眠ってしまうのは何故？

Chapter 2..p10

Bipedal Walking and Communication
二足歩行とコミュニケーションの関係性

Chapter 3..p17

The Male and Female Brain
男性と女性では脳の構造が違うの？

Health

Chapter 4..p24

The Five Tibetan Rites for Good Health
チベット体操が目指す健康法とは？

Chapter 5..p31

A Truly Bitter Medicinal Herb
アロエの凄さの秘密

Chapter 6..p38

The Healthiest Fruit?
キウイが一番健康によい果物か？

Technology

Chapter 7..p45

Life-changing Smart Devices
スマートマットレスと睡眠改善

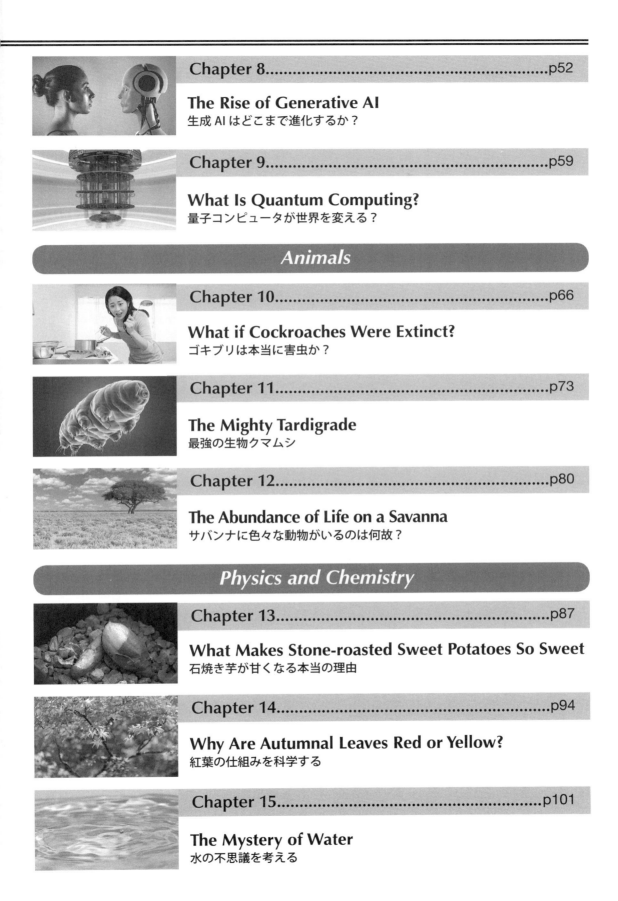

Chapter 8 .... p52

The Rise of Generative AI
生成 AI はどこまで進化するか？

Chapter 9 .... p59

What Is Quantum Computing?
量子コンピュータが世界を変える？

Animals

Chapter 10 .... p66

What if Cockroaches Were Extinct?
ゴキブリは本当に害虫か？

Chapter 11 .... p73

The Mighty Tardigrade
最強の生物クマムシ

Chapter 12 .... p80

The Abundance of Life on a Savanna
サバンナに色々な動物がいるのは何故？

Physics and Chemistry

Chapter 13 .... p87

What Makes Stone-roasted Sweet Potatoes So Sweet
石焼き芋が甘くなる本当の理由

Chapter 14 .... p94

Why Are Autumnal Leaves Red or Yellow?
紅葉の仕組みを科学する

Chapter 15 .... p101

The Mystery of Water
水の不思議を考える

vii

Humans

Chapter 1

Sleeping on Trains

電車内で眠ってしまうのは何故？

電車内で寝てしまったという経験は誰もが持っていますが、そもそもどうして寝てしまうのでしょうか。何が睡眠を誘うのでしょうか。電車内での温度？座席の心地よさ？電車内で睡眠を誘発する仕組みを科学してみましょう。

Vocabulary Check

1〜7の単語の意味を (a) 〜 (g) から選びましょう。

1. atmosphere
2. standout
3. fall asleep
4. drowsiness
5. subtle
6. replicate
7. apparatus

(a) something that is remarkably noticeable
(b) difficult to understand or perceive
(c) the character, feeling, or mood of a place or situation
(d) to make an exact copy of
(e) a device or equipment
(f) to start to sleep
(g) the state of feeling sleepy

Reading

Quite a few tourists in Japan are surprised to see the locals sleeping on trains. Perhaps because Japan is such a safe and well-mannered country, people of all ages are not at all concerned about sleeping on trains. Some even manage to sleep while standing. It might be that the environment inside trains creates an atmosphere almost as comfortable as their own bedrooms.

People tend to get sleepy not only on trains, but also on buses and in cars. Trains are a standout due to the seating arrangement being seemingly not conducive to sleeping. Some might fall asleep because the temperature inside the train is comfortable. Busy jobs and hectic schedules could contribute to others falling asleep. And others still may be tired from staying up all night studying or playing video games.

Professor Norio Inou from Institute of Science Tokyo started researching why his son always fell asleep during a particular section of his train route. He discovered that the cause of drowsiness varies depending on the train company and section, and it is due mostly to vibrations.

According to Professor Inou, vibrations of about 1Hz, which is one vibration per second, tend to induce sleep. Furthermore, he found that subtle vibrations, which are barely noticeable, are more likely to induce sleep than prominent ones. Research is currently being conducted to replicate these vibrations to promote better sleep quality.

When crying babies are rocked gently, they often stop crying. This is thought to be partly due to the shaking causing a type of vibration. However, it is unrealistic for a mother to hold and rock her baby all the time, so apparatuses that automatically rock babies are available. Similarly, when we lie in a hammock, we might quickly fall asleep, suggesting that moderate rocking or vibration can contribute to sleep.

People in need of sleep may want to know which railway company, which train car, and which section of a train route to ride to fall asleep more easily. Railway companies are constantly making every effort to improve ride quality. They work tirelessly to reduce the number of rail joints, change suspension systems, and adjust seats. As a result, even if a particular section has 1Hz vibrations during a study, it might change by the following week, or even the next day!

Notes

conducive 助けになる / hectic schedule 忙しいスケジュール / induce 誘発する / barely noticeable ほとんど気づかれない / prominent 顕著な / rock 赤ん坊を揺らす / hammock ハンモック / tirelessly 絶え間なく / suspension system 緩衝装置

Chapter 1　Sleeping on Trains

▶ Comprehension

１．次の文が本文の内容と一致する場合は T を、異なる場合は F を記入しましょう。

(1) [　　] It is uncommon to see people sleeping on trains in Japan.

(2) [　　] Vibrations of about 1Hz are more likely to keep people awake.

(3) [　　] Railway companies are always working to improve ride quality.

２．次の質問に対する答えとして最も適切なものを (A) ～ (D) の中から選びましょう。

(1) Why do people tend to get sleepy on trains, according to the passage?
    (A) Because of the seating arrangement
    (B) Due to vibrations mostly
    (C) Because trains are usually noisy
    (D) Due to the heat in the cars

(2) Which of the following is NOT mentioned as a factor contributing to sleepiness on trains?
    (A) Comfortable temperatures
    (B) Busy jobs and hectic schedules
    (C) Checking cellphones on the train
    (D) Staying up all night

(3) What is one way railway companies try to improve ride quality?
    (A) By changing the speed of trains
    (B) By adjusting seats and suspension systems
    (C) By reducing the number of train cars
    (D) By adding more rail joints

5

Grammar Points

前置詞

前置詞の意味：名詞句の前に置かれる品詞だから前置詞という。
超重要前置詞：of, at, on, in, from, to, for, by, with, intoの10個は頻出で最重要。
(1) ＜動詞＋前置詞＞の重要熟語例
　　⇒ contribute to ～（～に貢献する）、consist of ～（～から成る）など。
(2) ＜形容詞＋前置詞＞の重要熟語例
　　⇒ afraid of ～（～が怖い）、proportional to ～（～に比例する）など。
(3) ＜副詞＋前置詞＞の重要熟語例
　　⇒ away from ～（～から離れて）、according to ～（～によれば）など。
(4) 名詞と前置詞の関わりの重要な例
　　⇒ an interest in ～（～に対する関心）、as a result（結果として）など。
注意すべき前置詞の用法
(1) for A to do ～：不定詞の意味上の主語を表すのにforを用いる。A＝主語
(2) 大きな乗り物に乗る場合はon、小さな乗り物に乗る場合はinを用いる。
　　⇒ get on a bus/train/plane、get in a car/taxi

次の英文の ( ) 内に入る適切な語を (A)~(D) の中から選びましょう。

(1) People are prone to fall asleep not only on trains, but also on buses and (　　) cars.
　(A) by　　　(B) in　　　(C) into　　　(D) on

(2) Crammed schedules could contribute (　　) some people falling asleep.
　(A) that　　　(B) to　　　(C) what　　　(D) with

(3) The cause of sleepiness differs depending (　　) the railway company and train section.
　(A) at　　　(B) from　　　(C) in　　　(D) on

(4) According (　　) the professor, vibrations of about 1Hz are likely to cause drowsiness.
　(A) as　　　(B) that　　　(C) to　　　(D) with

(5) It is unrealistic (　　) a mother to carry her baby in her arms all the time.
　(A) for　　　(B) of　　　(C) that　　　(D) to

Composition Clues

次の英文の（　　）内の語(句)を並べ替えて、日本語訳に合う英文にしましょう。

(1) There are (a / few / new / quite / trains) in this city.
この都市にはかなりの数の新しい電車があります。
(　　　　　　　　　　　　　　　　　　　　　　　　　　　　　)

(2) Commuters (being / contribute / the / to / train) crowded.
通勤者が電車の混雑の一因となっています。
(　　　　　　　　　　　　　　　　　　　　　　　　　　　　　)

(3) Modern trains (also / are / but / fast / not only) comfortable.
現代の電車は速いだけでなく、快適でもあります。
(　　　　　　　　　　　　　　　　　　　　　　　　　　　　　)

(4) It is (asleep / common / fall / for passengers / to) during train journeys.
乗客が電車の旅の途中で眠ることはよくあります。
(　　　　　　　　　　　　　　　　　　　　　　　　　　　　　)

(5) A (be / is / likely / to / train) more crowded during rush hour.
電車はラッシュアワー中に混雑しやすいです。
(　　　　　　　　　　　　　　　　　　　　　　　　　　　　　)

Listening and Dictation

 1-08

次の本文の要約文を聞いて、空所に英単語を書き入れましょう。その後、その単語を下の枠内から選び、その記号で答えましょう。

　　　Many tourists in Japan are surprised to see the (1.　　　　) sleeping on trains. Actually, people of all (2.　　　　) sleep on trains in Japan. Some even manage to sleep (3.　　　　) standing. Good public safety and manners may (4.　　　　) to this.

　　　Trains are a (5.　　　　) because the seating (6.　　　　) is seemingly not suited to sleeping. Some might fall (7.　　　　) as the temperature inside the train is comfortable. Busy schedules could lead to others falling asleep. Professor Norio Inou from Institute of Science Tokyo started researching (8.　　　　) his son always fell asleep during a particular section of his train (9.　　　　). He discovered that the cause of drowsiness varies depending on the train company and section, and it is due mostly to (10.　　　　).

| (a) ages | (b) arrangement | (c) asleep | (d) contribute | (e) locals |
| (f) route | (g) standout | (h) vibrations | (i) while | (j) why |

科学よもやま話 1.　　電車と忘れ物

電車で寝てしまうことはよくありますが、忘れ物をしてしまうことはそれ以上に多いかもしれません。電車内で持ち主不明の傘を何度も目にしたことがあるかと思います。忘れ物で一番多いのは傘なのです。相鉄グループが公表しているデータでは、2021年度は、60,672件（約166件/日）の忘れ物があり、13,643件は傘です。それでは忘れ物ランキングトップ5を見ていきましょう。

1	傘	13,643件
2	現金	5,595件
3	袋・封筒類	4,561件
4	かばん類	3,464件
5	カードケース類	3,257件

Chapter 1 Sleeping on Trains

❯ Talk and Discussion

次の２つのトピックでトークまたはディスカッションをしましょう。

1. What kind of activities help you fall asleep?

_____

_____

2. Discuss the best ways to reduce stress in daily life.

_____

_____

🔍 ❯ *Useful Expressions*

(1) It is necessary for us to do … because ….. .

(2) I don't quite understand the point of your story when you say …. .

(3) I do two things to get rid of stress: One is …, and the other is …. .

(4) I partly agree with you, but I think …. .

(5) My opinion differs from yours to some extent. In my opinion, …. .

コミュニケーションのコツ **1.**　＜通時的方法と共時的方法＞

　ディスカッションの展開方法は、次の2つに大別でき、それぞれ主として2つに下位分類できる。

① **通時的方法（Diachronic Method）**

（ⅰ）時系列（time order）で展開する

　　トピックが時間の流れによってどのように変化するか、その過程に注目して意見表明を展開する。

（ⅱ）原因と結果(cause and effect)の視点から展開する

　　物事の原因と結果（トピックに関して、ある事象が何故起こったのかという点）に着目し、意見表明を展開する。

② **共時的方法（Synchronic Method）**

（ⅰ）列挙(listing)と分類(classification)の視点から展開する

　　トピックに関するものを単に挙げて論じることを「列挙」、幾つかのグループに分けて論じることを「分類」といい、これらの視点から意見表明を展開する。

（ⅱ）比較(comparison)と対比(contrast)の視点から展開する

　　似ている点を比べるのを「比較」、違う点を比べるのを「対比」といい、これらの視点から意見表明を展開する。

9

Humans

Chapter 2
Bipedal Walking and Communication

二足歩行とコミュニケーションの関係性

カンガルーは二足歩行する動物と言えます。人間の二足歩行とどう違うのでしょうか。言葉によるコミュニケーションは、他の動物にはない人間だけの特徴です。人間の二足歩行とコミュニケーションには関係がありそうです。

▶ Vocabulary Check

1～7の単語の意味を (a) ～ (g) から選びましょう。

1. upright   (a) to be greater or more important than something else
2. trait   (b) not anticipated
3. lung   (c) an organ used for breathing
4. unexpected   (d) possibly not true or correct
5. sedentary   (e) straight or vertical
6. outweigh   (f) a lifestyle with little physical activity
7. arguably   (g) a characteristic or feature

Reading

We take upright bipedal walking for granted, but among animals, it is a unique trait. Our ability to walk upright on two legs is thanks to our pelvis and foot arches. The pelvis is bowl-shaped, supporting the heavy weight of our internal organs. Additionally, the arches in our feet develop muscles that work to support the upper body.

You might think that kangaroos and birds also walk on two legs. It is true that kangaroos and birds do indeed walk on two legs, but they do not walk upright. To walk upright means that the torso is perpendicular to the ground. Taking this into consideration, a human being is the only animal that can truly walk upright on two legs.

There is no doubt that upright bipedal walking brought about many conveniences. By freeing up the hands, humans could carry objects. But that's not the only advantage. It is believed that our ability to speak is also a benefit unintentionally brought about by upright bipedal walking. At face value, it may seem that walking upright has nothing to do with speaking, but they are in fact closely related.

To produce speech, air pushed from the lungs vibrates the vocal cords, and the tongue and lips control the airflow. Unlike other animals, humans have a vertical airway and esophagus that connect directly. This allows us to push out enough air to speak.

While upright bipedal walking brought unexpected benefits, it also came with disadvantages, such as back pain. Previously, forces acted horizontally, but now all forces act vertically, increasing the strain on our backs. Developing muscles can help, but many modern humans have sedentary lifestyles, spending much time sitting, so muscles do not develop naturally. In addition, the change in pelvis shape led to more difficult childbirth.

It's unclear whether the advantages of upright bipedal walking outweigh the disadvantages, like back pain and harder childbirth, but the ability to speak is without doubt significant. The ability to communicate with language is arguably humanity's greatest tool. A seemingly simple daily activity such as walking and talking with a friend with a cup of coffee in one hand is a uniquely human action due to the benefits of being an upright bipedal species.

Notes

bipedal walking 二足歩行 / pelvis 骨盤 / internal organ 内臓 / torso 胴体 / perpendicular 垂直の / at face value 額面どおりに / vibrate 振動する / vocal cord 声帯 / vertical airway 垂直の気道 / esophagus 食道 / strain 負担

❯ Comprehension

1．次の文が本文の内容と一致する場合は T を、異なる場合は F を記入しましょう。

(1) [　　] Humans are the only animals that can walk upright on two legs.

(2) [　　] The vertical airway and esophagus in humans are unrelated to our ability to speak.

(3) [　　] Upright bipedal walking has brought only advantages to humans.

2．次の質問に対する答えとして最も適切なものを (A)〜(D) の中から選びましょう。

(1) What allows humans to walk upright on two legs?

(A) Strong arm muscles

(B) Bowl-shaped pelvis and foot arches

(C) Sedentary lifestyles

(D) Large internal organs

(2) Which of the following is NOT mentioned as a result of upright bipedal walking?

(A) Ability to carry objects

(B) Ease of producing speech sounds

(C) Increased risk of heart disease

(D) Back pain

(3) What is a significant disadvantage of upright bipedal walking?

(A) Lack of communication skills

(B) Easier childbirth

(C) Increased back strain

(D) Less muscle development

Chapter 2　Bipedal Walking and Communication

 Grammar Points

不定詞

不定詞の形：to＋動詞の原形
不定詞の用法
(1) 名詞用法：「～すること」⇒ 主語、目的語、または、補語となる。
(2) 形容詞用法：「～するための」⇒ ＜名詞句＋to do ～＞の形となる。
(3) 副詞用法：「～するために」⇒ 文頭、または、動詞句の語尾に来る。
不定詞の使用に関する注意事項
(1) 不定詞を目的語にとる動詞と動名詞を目的語にとる動詞がある。
　　不定詞：hope to do、wish to do、want to do、promise to do、plan to doなど。
　　動名詞：enjoy doing、avoid doing、finish doing、spend time doing ～など。
(2) 等位接続詞で結ぶ場合、同じ形となるようにする。名詞用法が共通していても形を揃えることが必要。
　　⇒ ○eating and drinking　/　✕eating and to drink

次の英文の（　）内に入る適切な語（句）を (A)~(D) の中から選びましょう。

(1) (　　　) upright means that a person stands vertically to the ground.
　(A) To walk　　　(B) Walk　　　(C) Walked　　　(D) Walks

(2) Humans' ability (　　　) is a benefit brought by upright bipedal walking.
　(A) in speaking　　　　　(B) for speaking
　(C) of speaking　　　　　(D) to speak

(3) (　　　) speech, humans use the air pushed from the lungs to vibrate the vocal cords.
　(A) Produce　　(B) Produced　　(C) Producing　　(D) To produce

(4) Many people today tend to lead a sedentary life, spending much time (　　　).
　(A) sat　　　(B) sit　　　(C) sitting　　　(D) to sit

(5) A simple everyday activity like walking and (　　　) with a friend with a cup of coffee in one hand is said to be a uniquely human action.
　(A) talk　　　(B) talked　　　(C) talking　　　(D) to talk

❯ Composition Clues

次の英文の（　　　）内の語（句）を並べ替えて、日本語訳に合う英文にしましょう。

(1) Many people (bipedalism / for / granted / simply / take).
多くの人々は二足歩行を当然のことと思っています。
(　　　　　　　　　　　　　　　　　　　　　　　　　　　　　　　　　　)

(2) Humans can walk long distances (bipedal / efficiency / thanks / their / to).
人間は二足歩行のおかげで長距離を歩くことができます。
(　　　　　　　　　　　　　　　　　　　　　　　　　　　　　　　　　　)

(3) (is / it / that / though / true) walking on two legs increases visibility, it also has drawbacks.
二足歩行は視界を良くするのは事実ですが、それには欠点もあります。
(　　　　　　　　　　　　　　　　　　　　　　　　　　　　　　　　　　)
＊ 文頭に置かれる単語であっても小文字になっています

(4) (doubt / is / no / that / there) bipedalism has been crucial to human development.
二足歩行が人間の発展にとって重要であったことは間違いありません。
(　　　　　　　　　　　　　　　　　　　　　　　　　　　　　　　　　　)
＊ 文頭に置かれる単語であっても小文字になっています

(5) When we compare different forms of locomotion, we see that (of / bipedalism / outweigh / the advantages / the disadvantages).
様々な形の移動方法を比較すると、二足歩行の利点が欠点を上回っていることが分かります。
(　　　　　　　　　　　　　　　　　　　　　　　　　　　　　　　　　　)

Chapter 2 Bipedal Walking and Communication

● Listening and Dictation

🎧 1-15

次の本文の要約文を聞いて、空所に英単語を書き入れましょう。その後、その単語を下の枠内から選び、その記号で答えましょう。

We take (1.) bipedal walking for (2.), but among animals, it is a unique (3.). Our ability to walk upright on two legs is thanks to our pelvis and foot (4.). The pelvis is bowl-shaped, supporting the heavy (5.) of our internal (6.). Additionally, the arches in our feet develop (7.) that work to support the (8.) body. You might think that kangaroos and birds also walk on two legs. It is true that kangaroos and (9.) do indeed walk on two legs, but they do not walk upright. To walk upright means that the torso is perpendicular to the ground. Taking this into (10.), we are the only animal that can truly walk upright on two legs.

(a) arches	(b) birds	(c) consideration	(d) granted	(e) muscles
(f) organs	(g) trait	(h) upper	(i) upright	(j) weight

科学よもやま話 2.　　二足歩行がもたらしたもの

　地球上に生命が誕生したのは約40億年前のことです。約600万年前に誕生した類人猿も二足歩行をしていた可能性がありますが、約300万年前に完全な直立二足歩行になったようです。

　二足歩行になると胎盤が狭くなるので、必然的に赤ん坊を未熟児で産むことになります。すると、赤ん坊とコミュニケーションをとらないといけない状況が生じます。二足歩行の体型で、ちょうど声帯が発達し、都合がよく言語能力が発達することになりました。

　そもそもどうして直立二足歩行となったのかについては諸説ありますが、「運搬説」（物を運び易く進化したという説）が有力です。立っていた方が物を運び易いのは間違いありません。オスがメスに食べ物を運んで、メスの気を引くこと（プレゼント仮説）や、子育てを一緒にすること（子育て仮説）とも関係がありそうです。

▶ Talk and Discussion

次の2つのトピックでトークまたはディスカッションをしましょう。

1. What do you think makes humans so different from other animals, and why?

_____

_____

2. How would your life change if you had to get around on your hands and feet like a dog?

_____

_____

Useful Expressions

(1) There is an interesting story about it, which recounts that ….． .
(2) It plays the most important role in the human body because ….． .
(3) The same can be said about ….． .
(4) There is always a clash of opinions about ….． .
(5) My opinion is entirely different from yours. I think ….． .

コミュニケーションのコツ 2.　＜思考を柔軟にする＞

次の問題を解ける?
April has 30 days. May has 31 days. Then which month has 28 days?
(4月は30日、5月は31日あります。ではどの月が28日あるでしょうか。)

　答えは、every month。Februaryではない。というのは、どの月も28日間を含むからである。一般にX has Y. は X>Yということになるので、28日間を含んでいるのは、2月だけではない。

　ここで、質問が、Which month has only 28 days?(28日しかないのはどの月でしょうか?)というようにonlyが入っていると、答えはFebruaryになる。

　頭の柔らかさが問われるのであるが、これも論理的な批判力があれば問題ない。論理的な感性を研ぎ澄ませて、論理的批判力を高めよう。

Humans

Chapter 3
The Male and Female Brain

男性と女性では脳の構造が違うの？

脳は現在でも十分に解明されていないようです。脳の大きさと賢さには関係があるのでしょうか。男性の脳と女性の脳は異なるのでしょうか。いろいろと疑問が湧いてきますが、ここでは、男女の脳にどのような違いがあるのか、一歩進んで学びます。

▶ Vocabulary Check

1～7の単語の意味を (a) ～ (g) から選びましょう。

1. correlate   (a) to make easier or assist
2. perceive   (b) a person's character or disposition
3. facilitate   (c) to see or notice
4. comprehensive   (d) existing as an idea only
5. widespread   (e) covering all or nearly all elements or aspects
6. nature   (f) to have a related connection
7. abstract   (g) existing or happening in many places

Reading

🎧 CD 1-16〜20

People often wonder whether the brain sizes between men and women differ. Generally, men have larger bodies and weigh more compared to women. If brain sizes were proportional to body weight, it would mean that most men have larger brains than women. However, having a larger brain does not necessarily mean being smarter. For example, sumo wrestlers

5　are often massive, but this doesn't mean they are much smarter than smaller individuals. The sperm whale, which is about 20 meters long and weighs around 60 tons, has a brain weighing approximately 10 kilograms. In contrast, an adult human male's brain weighs about 1.4 kilograms. We cannot conclude that sperm whales are seven times as smart as humans. While there is a difference in brain size between men and women, it does not

10　correlate with intelligence.

However, there are differences in the brains of men and women. Men's brains tend to have denser connections between the front and back. This suggests a higher ability to perceive surroundings. On the other hand, women's brains have denser connections between the right and left hemispheres. This is believed to facilitate better information gathering and

15　comprehensive decision-making. These ideas lead to debate, with some arguing that any differences might be due to environmental factors or personality traits rather than differences in sex.

Unfortunately, terms like "male brain" and "female brain" are widespread, similar to "right-brained" or "left-brained" concepts, but they don't actually exist. For instance, even

20　if differences are observed in brain scans of men and women in their 30s, it cannot be definitively concluded that these differences are due to sex. The brain is influenced by both genetics and other factors.

Research suggests that personality differences are more significant than differences in sex. Extroverted and curious people tend to have a thinner but broader cerebral cortex,

25　indicating more neurons. Conversely, nervous individuals have a thicker but smaller cerebral cortex. Additionally, people with an introverted nature have larger and thicker gray matter in the prefrontal cortex, responsible for abstract thinking, compared to extroverts. This suggests that introverts spend more time on abstract thinking.

We should focus less on gender stereotypes and more on environmental factors such as

30　social structures when considering brain differences. Understanding that the brain is shaped by both biological and social influences can help us appreciate the complexity of human behavior beyond simple gender categories.

Notes ●●

sperm whale マッコウクジラ / denser connection 密な接続 / right and left hemispheres 右脳と左脳の半球 / extroverted 外交的な / thinner 薄い / cerebral cortex 大脳皮質 / neurons 神経細胞 / introverted 内向的な / gray matter 灰白質 / prefrontal cortex 前頭前野 / gender stereotype 性別固定観念

Chapter 3 The Male and Female Brain

❯ Comprehension

１．次の文が本文の内容と一致する場合は T を、異なる場合は F を記入しましょう。

(1) [　　] Generally, men have smaller brains than women due to their body size.

(2) [　　] Brain size differences between men and women correlate with intelligence.

(3) [　　] Personality differences are suggested to be more significant than sex differences in brain structure.

２．次の質問に対する答えとして最も適切なものを (A) 〜 (D) の中から選びましょう。

(1) What does the denser connection between the front and back of men's brains suggest?

(A) Better abstract thinking

(B) Enhanced ability to perceive surroundings

(C) Improved memory retention

(D) Greater emotional sensitivity

(2) Which of the following is NOT mentioned as a concept related to "male brain" and "female brain"?

(A) Left-brained

(B) Right-brained

(C) Top-brained

(D) Gender stereotypes

(3) What is indicated by a thinner but broader cerebral cortex?

(A) More neurons

(B) Fewer neurons

(C) Larger prefrontal cortex

(D) Thicker gray matter

19

Grammar Points

比較

比較の表現：3つの形がある。（品詞は形容詞と副詞の2つにこの表現がある）
　(1)原級：形容詞・副詞のもとの形→ as ～ as A（Aと同じ）
　(2)比較級：短い場合（通例単音節）→ ～ er than A（Aよりも～）
　　　　　　長い場合（2音節以上）→ more ～ than A（Aよりも～）
　(3)最上級：短い場合（通例単音節）→ ～ est of A（Aのうち最も～）
　　　　　　長い場合（2音節以上）→ the most ～ of A（Aのうち最も～）

比較で注意すべきこと
　(1)強調する場合：比較級にmuch, far, evenを付ける。→ far larger
　　　　　　　　　最上級に by far を付ける。→ by far the best
　(2)倍数比較：N times as ～ as A（AのN倍～である）
　　注：N timesの後に比較級を続けてもよい。
　(3) most ～ s で「たいていの～」の意味、mostだけで「たいていの人」の意味。
　(4) A rather than Bで「BというよりはむしろA」という意味。

次の英文の（　）内に入る適切な語（句）を (A)~(D) の中から選びましょう。

(1) If brain sizes were in proportion to body weight, it would imply that (　　) men have larger brains than women.

　　(A) few more　　(B) more than　　(C) most　　(D) the most

(2) Average sumo wrestlers weigh 162 kg, but this doesn't mean they are (　　) slimmer people.

　　(A) by far the smartest of　　(B) far smarter than
　　(C) the smarter of the two　　(D) too smarter than

(3) We haven't come to the conclusion that whales are seven times (　　) humans.

　　(A) as smart as　　(B) more smart　　(C) smarter　　(D) the smartest

(4) Differences due to environmental factors can be found (　　) than those of sex.

　　(A) better　　(B) fewer　　(C) further　　(D) rather

(5) Some people focus more on environmental factors but (　　) on gender stereotypes.

　　(A) least　　(B) less　　(C) lesser　　(D) littler

Composition Clues

次の英文の（　　）内の語(句)を並べ替えて、日本語訳に合う英文にしましょう。

(1) Scientists (brain / compared / human / the / to) those of other species.
科学者たちは人間の脳を他の種と比較しました。
(　　　　　　　　　　　　　　　　　　　　　　　　　　　　　　　　　　)

(2) Some researchers (focus / how / memory / on / works).
一部の研究者は記憶の働きに注目しています。
(　　　　　　　　　　　　　　　　　　　　　　　　　　　　　　　　　　)

(3) People (are / have / larger brains / not / who) necessarily smarter.
脳が大きい人が必ずしも賢いわけではありません。
(　　　　　　　　　　　　　　　　　　　　　　　　　　　　　　　　　　)

(4) Adults tend to put (contrast / effort / in / into / solving problems) with children.
大人は子供とは対照的に問題を解決しようと努力する傾向があります。
(　　　　　　　　　　　　　　　　　　　　　　　　　　　　　　　　　　)

(5) When studying the brain, one might (affects / behavior / whether / wonder / size).
脳を研究する際、大きさが行動に影響を与えるかどうか疑問に思うかもしれません。
(　　　　　　　　　　　　　　　　　　　　　　　　　　　　　　　　　　)

Listening and Dictation

次の本文の要約文を聞いて、空所に英単語を書き入れましょう。その後、その単語を下の枠内から選び、その記号で答えましょう。

　　　People want to know (1.　　　　　) the brain sizes between men and women differ. Generally, men (2.　　　　　) more than women; therefore, most men have (3.　　　　　) brains than women. However, this fact does not (4.　　　　　) imply that men are wiser. The 20-meter-long sperm (5.　　　　　), which weighs around 60 tons, has a ten-kilogram brain. On the other hand, an (6.　　　　　) human (7.　　　　　) brain weighs about (8.　　　　　) kilograms. However, we cannot say that sperm whales are seven times cleverer than humans.

　　　Men's brains have a tendency to have denser connections between the front and back, while women's brains have denser connections between the right and left (9.　　　　　). Some argue that brain differences may be based on environmental factors or personality (10.　　　　　) rather than differences of sex.

(a) 1.4	(b) adult	(c) hemispheres	(d) larger	(e) male's
(f) necessarily	(g) traits	(h) weigh	(i) whale	(j) whether

科学よもやま話 3.　　脳の活動を垣間見る

　脳は私たちの体重の約2％しか占めていませんが、エネルギーの約20％を消費します。この高エネルギー消費は、脳が絶え間なく情報を処理し、活動を維持していることを示しています。寝ている間でさえしっかりと仕事をしてくれています。脳がそれだけエネルギーを消費するということは、ケーキやドーナツを食べても、脳をフル回転させれば太らないのではと思うかもしれませんが、世の中そんなに甘くはありません。脳がエネルギーにできるのはブドウ糖だけです。脂肪はしっかりとおなかに蓄えられてしまいますので食べすぎにご注意ください。

エネルギー消費量が多い臓器

1. 肝臓：約27％　　2. 脳：約20％　　3. 骨格筋：約18％
4. 腎臓：約10％　　5. 心臓：約7％

Chapter 3 The Male and Female Brain

❯ Talk and Discussion

次の2つのトピックでトークまたはディスカッションをしましょう。

1. What are the greatest differences between men and women?

_____

_____

· ·

2. Are the differences between men and women mainly due to brain structure or social influences?

_____

_____

Useful Expressions

(1) Those that distinguish between men and women include .... .

(2) There are a lot of differences between them; one of them is .... .

(3) There is some truth in what you say, but I dare say .... .

(4) I want to place emphasis on .... . [=I want to stress that .... .]

(5) By taking this opportunity, I would like to say .... .

コミュニケーションのコツ **3.** ＜表現を変えてみる＞

　英語は同義語が多いのが特徴です。例えば、「素晴らしい」という意味の単語を挙げると、wonderful, splendid, superb, magnificent, [女性がよく使う] marvelousなどがあります。口語では、great, fine, terrific, amazing, fantastic, fabulous, awful, stunningなどもあり、英語の凄さを感じることができます。

　いつも、greatやfineだけを使うのではなく、色々な表現を使うことが、気持ちのよいコミュニケーションを円滑に行うコツと言えるでしょう。

　このことは、構文にも言えます。いつも同じ構文を使うのではなく、同じ文でも幾つかの表現方法を知っていることも必要でしょう。

It is important to study English in Japan. 　　（日本では英語の勉強は重要です。）
It is English that we should study in Japan. 　（日本で勉強すべきなのは英語です。）
What is important in Japan is English study. 　（日本で重要なのは英語の勉強です。）
In Japan, the important thing is to study English. （日本で、重要なのは英語の勉強です。）

23

Health

Chapter 4
The Five Tibetan Rites for Good Health

チベット体操が目指す健康法とは？

適度な運動が心身の健康を保つのに重要であることは昔から言われています。ヨガや気功なども健康法として有名ですね。ここでは、ちょっと珍しいエクササイズであるチベット体操について、その奥深さを感じてみたいと思います。

▶ Vocabulary Check

1〜7の単語の意味を (a) 〜 (g) から選びましょう。

1. vitality
2. esoteric
3. aging
4. rotate
5. affect
6. profound
7. depletion

(a) becoming older and older
(b) great energy and eagerness to do things
(c) known or understood by only a few people
(d) the situation where something is nearly all used up
(e) having a strong and outstanding influence
(f) to turn with a circular movement around a central point
(g) to do something that causes an effect on something

 Exercises such as yoga, meditation, and Qigong (*Kiko* in Japanese) are currently popular. One common feature is the incorporation of breathing control with simple physical exercise, leading to greater vitality while relieving muscle stiffness. Of particular interest are a series of Tibetan exercises known as the "Five Tibetan Rites."

 The Five Tibetan Rites contain the above-mentioned aspects of yoga and meditation, for those who want to train themselves both physically and mentally. What distinguishes these exercises is their spiritual aspect. The exercises, which are steeped in the ideas of esoteric Tibetan Buddhism, consist of five "rituals," meaning five different bodily motions that incorporate breathing control through meditation.

 Tibetan Buddhism has many secrets which were not introduced into China or Japan. Its mysteries developed organically without foreign influence. One of its secrets, the Five Tibetan Rites, has been taught by Tibetan spiritual guides, or lamas, for centuries.

 According to Tibetan Buddhism, the debilitating effects of aging are caused by a disruption in the circulation of a person's life energy. This energy is called *lung*, which is pronounced "loong." Tibetan exercises seek to improve the flow of *lung*. Therefore, these exercises help rejuvenate and revitalize the body.

 Chakras are the body's primary energy centers, governing the proper function of our internal organs. The human body contains seven major chakras, which can be thought of as spinning wheels of energy. They contribute to our health when they are well-balanced and rotating at high speeds, or "open." Diseases are caused when chakras are unbalanced, or rotate slowly. In other words, they are "closed."

 The simple act of bending backwards and returning to an upright position stimulates the chakras that lack energy. This leads to faster rotation, promoting the smooth flow of *lung*. The first chakra, located at the base of the tailbone, is mainly affected by this exercise. During this exercise, the chakras located above gradually start to benefit from better energy flow.

 Deep breathing also has a profound effect on the chakras. Tibetan Buddhism teaches a breathing technique known as *pranayama*. This practice of deep and slow meditative breathing helps channel vital energy, further stimulating the chakras.

 Ultimately, the Five Tibetan Rites seek to reverse energy depletion. Loss of energy is caused by unbalanced or slowly rotating chakras. As these Tibetan exercises help cleanse and revitalize the chakras to restore energy, they may help us retain youthful energy and exuberance, even as we age.

Notes

Qigong 気功 / Tibetan Rites チベットの儀式 / steeped in 〜に包まれた、〜が浸透した / breathing control through meditation 瞑想の呼吸 / Tibetan spiritual guide チベットの霊的指導者 / lama チベット仏教における高位の僧や霊的指導者に対する敬称 / debilitating 衰弱させる / rejuvenate 若返らせる / revitalize 活性化する / chakra チャクラ / tailbone 尾てい骨 / channel 流す、運ぶ / exuberance 活気

❯ Comprehension

１．次の文が本文の内容と一致する場合は T を、異なる場合は F を記入しましょう。

(1) [　　　] What is incorporated into yoga, meditation, and Qigong is breathing control.

(2) [　　　] The Tibetan exercises are not at all related to esoteric Tibetan Buddhism.

(3) [　　　] The Five Tibetan Rites have been taught by esoteric Buddhist monks in China.

２．次の質問に対する答えとして最も適切なものを (A) ～ (D) の中から選びましょう。

(1) What is the cause of disease according to this passage?

(A) The debilitating effects of aging

(B) The improper function of our internal organs

(C) Unbalanced or slowly rotating chakras

(D) The simple act of bending backwards too much

(2) Which is the correct description of chakras?

(A) They are secondary centers of energy.

(B) They contribute to our health when they are well-balanced and rotating quickly.

(C) Tibetan exercise will first affect the chakra located at the lower part of the body.

(D) It is meditation, not breathing, that has a strong influence on the chakras.

(3) Which statement most correctly reflects information from the passage?

(A) The Five Tibetan Rites contain aspects of meditation unrelated to yoga.

(B) The breathing during Tibetan exercise is based on Qigong.

(C) The practice of deep and rapid breathing stimulates the chakras.

(D) Unbalanced or slowly rotating chakras will cause a loss of energy.

Grammar Points

句と節

1. **句：主語と動詞の構造がない語のまとまり**
   名詞句・形容詞句・副詞句がある。
   ・不定詞(to do形)は、名詞用法・形容詞用法・副詞用法がある。
   ・動名詞(doing形)は名詞句、分詞(doing形とdone形)は形容詞句を作る。
   ・前置詞は、形容詞句と副詞句を作る。（共に前置詞句ということもある。）

2. **節：主語と動詞の構造がある語のまとまり**
   名詞節・形容詞節・副詞節がある。
   ・thatとwhether(接続詞)、疑問詞の全てと関係詞のwhatは名詞節を作る。
   ・関係詞のwhat以外は、全て形容詞節を作る。（先行詞を形容する。）
   ・接続詞(上記以外：例えばwhen, while, because, since)は副詞節を作る。

次の英文の(　)内に入る適切な語(句)を(A)~(D)の中から選びましょう。

(1) (　　　) is common to physical exercises for good health is the incorporation of breathing control into their routines.
 (A) As   (B) One   (C) That   (D) What

(2) (　　　) particular interest is the fact that many of the exercises have an aspect of meditation as part of their training processes.
 (A) Of   (B) So   (C) Very   (D) Whether

(3) The health-promoting project (　　　) 50 trained staff members is hard to carry out in my view.
 (A) involve   (B) involved   (C) involves   (D) involving

(4) Since I want to live to be older than 100, (　　　) of the body may be of prime importance.
 (A) revitalize   (B) to revitalize   (C) the revitalizing   (D) which revitalization

(5) If you continue to do this physical exercise, you will spiritually grow younger, even as you (　　　).
 (A) age   (B) aged   (C) aging   (D) will age

❯ Composition Clues

次の英文の（　　　　）内の語を並べ替えて、日本語訳に合う英文にしましょう。

(1) (an / aura / is / of / there) mystery about the meditation-based breathing method.
瞑想を基本とした呼吸法には不思議な雰囲気が漂っています。

(　　　　　　　　　　　　　　　　　　　　　　　　　　　　　　　　　　　)

＊文頭に置かれる単語であっても小文字になっています

(2) The special meditation centering on the first letter of Sanskrit (ideas / in / is / steeped / the) of esoteric Shingon Buddhism.
サンスクリット語の阿を中心とする特別の瞑想法（阿字観）は真言密教の考えが浸透しています。

(　　　　　　　　　　　　　　　　　　　　　　　　　　　　　　　　　　　)

(3) The smooth flow of energy (as / is / of / the / thought) result of chakras rotating rapidly.
エネルギーのスムーズな流れは、チャクラが高速回転している結果と考えられます。

(　　　　　　　　　　　　　　　　　　　　　　　　　　　　　　　　　　　)

(4) The revitalization of the chakras (a / effect / has / on / profound) the restoration of our body's energy.
チャクラの活性化は我々の体のエネルギーの回復に多大な効果があります。

(　　　　　　　　　　　　　　　　　　　　　　　　　　　　　　　　　　　)

(5) We can say that yoga is a physical exercise (helps / retain / that / us / youthful) energy to make us look younger.
ヨガは若いエネルギーを保ち、若く見えるようになるのに役立つ運動と言えます。

(　　　　　　　　　　　　　　　　　　　　　　　　　　　　　　　　　　　)

28

Chapter 4　The Five Tibetan Rites for Good Health

▶ Listening and Dictation

次の本文の要約文を聞いて、空所に英単語を書き入れましょう。その後、その単語を下の枠内から選び、その記号で答えましょう。

　　　　　Yoga and (1.　　　　　) are popular these days. Likewise, Tibetan exercises in particular (2.　　　　　) health through specific physical and mental activities. The Five Tibetan Rites have (3.　　　　　) been conducted by Tibetan spiritual guides known as lamas. They are (4.　　　　　) of five physical movements and one special breathing method. Poor (5.　　　　　) of a body's vital energy leads to our bodies becoming (6.　　　　　). The Five Rites seek to improve the circulation of this energy.

　　　　In our body there are (7.　　　　　) main chakras. When these chakras are open, we are healthy. Tibetan exercises accomplish this by promoting balanced chakras (8.　　　　　) at high speeds. If the rotation of chakras is (9.　　　　　) or low in speed, illness results. The Tibetan exercises, therefore, focus on restoring (10.　　　　　) energy through the healthy functioning of the chakras.

(a) circulation	(b) composed	(c) improve	(d) infirm	(e) long
(f) meditation	(g) rotating	(h) seven	(i) unbalanced	(j) youthful

科学よもやま話 4.　　7つのチャクラについて

- **第1チャクラ**（尾骨部）　人間が生きるうえで最も重要な「生存」チャクラです。ここが弱いと疲れやすくなり、強化されるとやる気が漲ります。
- **第2チャクラ**（丹田［＝おへそから指4本分下］）　「情愛」のチャクラです。ここが弱いと異性への興味が湧かなくなります。強化されると一層魅力的になります。
- **第3チャクラ**（みぞおちの少し下）　「権力や名誉」のチャクラです。ここが弱いと愚痴っぽくなったり、周りに無関心になりますが、強化されると実力が発揮できます。
- **第4チャクラ**（胸の中央）　「人類愛」のチャクラです。ここが弱いとマイナス思考になりやすくなりますが、強化されると人の役に立ちたいという意識が強くなります。
- **第5チャクラ**（喉）　「芸術」のチャクラです。ここが弱いと想像力や創造力が働かなくなりますが、強化されると音楽や美術など芸術面での才能が開花します。
- **第6チャクラ**（眉間）　「直感力」のチャクラです。ここが弱いと集中力がなくなり、考えがまとまらなくなります。強化されると勘が鋭くなります。
- **第7チャクラ**（頭頂部）　「統合」のチャクラです。人格と霊性を統合して、魂の本質的な生き方ができるようになります。

▶ Talk and Discussion

次の2つのトピックでトークまたはディスカッションをしましょう。

1. What kind of exercise do you do to maintain your health?

_____
_____

2. Do you think that traditional practices such as yoga and meditation can benefit our health? Why or why not?

_____
_____

Useful Expressions

(1) The exercise that I think is effective is …. .
(2) There are many things I want to say about this, but I will focus on …. .
(3) As for this problem, I especially want to say …. .
(4) To the best of my knowledge, …. .
(5) When it comes to having this type of situation, I would say …. .

コミュニケーションのコツ 4.　＜語法に気を付ける＞

　introduce（紹介する）という動詞に注目しましょう。（AにBを）与える[give]、送る[send]、教える[teach]のような第4文型（SVOO）の形式が使える動詞と同じように、「AにBを紹介する」と言えるので、「introduceも第4文型が使える」と考えてはいけません。
　この動詞は、「introduce B to A」のような形、すなわち、第3文型でしか使えません。単語の使い方（＝語法）に注意しましょう。例えば、「私はあなたにその考えを紹介します。」の英語は次のようになります。
○I will introduce the idea to you.
×I will introduce you the idea.

　因みに、語法を無視した次の英文も間違い例です。
×I will introduce about my way of keeping fit.　（私の健康法について紹介します。）
○Let me introduce my way of keeping fit to you.　（私の健康法を紹介します。）
　「〜について」に引っ張られて、aboutを付けてしまってはいけないのです。

Health

Chapter 5
A Truly Bitter Medicinal Herb

アロエの凄さの秘密

> 昔から「良薬は口に苦し」と言います。**bitter** なもの（苦いアロエ）は、**better** なもの（より良い植物）ということなのでしょう。実際、アロエは万能薬と言っても過言ではないぐらい、様々な効能があります。いろんな視点から、アロエの不思議を紐解きましょう。

▶ Vocabulary Check

1〜7 の単語の意味を (a)〜(g) から選びましょう。

1. impressive
2. specific
3. ingredient
4. compound
5. discharge
6. upheaval
7. abundance

(a) a chemical that combines two or more elements
(b) a phenomenon of something being pushed upward
(c) possessing a trait which is greatly admired
(d) relating to one thing, not others
(e) to send out a substance, especially liquid or gas
(f) the situation in which there is more than enough of something
(g) a part of something that is useful for a particular purpose

Reading

Aloe has been used as a folk remedy in Japan for centuries. The plant's healing powers are so impressive that some consider it almost mystical. It has long been said to be good for burns, cuts, and insect bites. In fact, aloe's medical benefits have been universally known since antiquity, even appearing in the Bible.

Aloe belongs to the lily family of plants along with onions, leeks, garlic, and asparagus. Despite its appearance and texture, aloe is not a member of the cactus family, as many believe. There are actually 300 to 500 kinds of aloe in the world. Only six or seven are now used in medicine, food, and cosmetics. Among these, aloe vera is one of the most popular species.

The words "aloe vera" contain a hint to the plant's effectiveness and taste. The Arabic word "alloe," meaning bitter, became "aloe." The Latin word "vera" means truth. This seems to indicate that aloe vera is the truest plant in terms of health, though it tastes bitter, as many medicines do.

Aloe vera is found in very specific regions, and generally speaking, grows best in subtropical zones. The climate in the southern parts of the Arabian Peninsula and the Mediterranean coasts of North Africa is particularly favorable for its growth.

Aloe vera contains 200 active ingredients, which work in harmony in a slightly acidic base. The resulting nutritional compound works mostly to strengthen the human immune system.

The plant's main ingredient is polysaccharide, which helps protect mucous membranes. It also prevents viral infection and helps produce collagen and hyaluronic acid. This active ingredient also sticks to toxic substances and bodily waste, and discharges them, performing a type of detox. The polysaccharide also promotes good bacteria growth in the bowels.

Aloe vera is especially effective in solving three important problems. It helps remove wrinkles and bags under eyes, which make people look younger; it also repairs the walls of blood vessels, leading to healthier blood circulation; finally, it can increase bone density, making people more physically resilient. We could say that aloe vera is practically a cure-all.

In Japan, aloe vera grows best on Miyako-jima Island in Okinawa Prefecture. This landmass was formed through the upheaval of coral reefs; therefore, the island is rich in coral limestone, alkaline soil, and an abundance of minerals, which all support the growth of high-quality aloe vera.

Notes

folk remedy 民間療法 / since antiquity 大昔から / lily family ユリ科 / leek ニラネギ / cactus family サボテン科 / aloe vera アロエベラ / subtropical zone 亜熱帯 / the Arabian Peninsula アラビア半島 / Mediterranean 地中海の / active ingredient 有効成分 / acidic base 酸性の環境 / immune system 免疫系 / polysaccharide 多糖体 / mucous membrane 粘膜 / viral infection ウイルス感染 / collagen コラーゲン / hyaluronic acid ヒアルロン酸 / bowel 腸 / bags under eyes 目の下のたるみ / bone density 骨密度 / resilient 回復力のある / cure-all 万能薬 / landmass 陸塊 / coral reef サンゴ礁 / coral limestone サンゴ石灰岩 / alkaline soil アルカリ性土壌

Chapter 5　A Truly Bitter Medicinal Herb

❯ Comprehension

１．次の文が本文の内容と一致する場合は T を、異なる場合は F を記入しましょう。

(1) [　　　] Aloe has long been used for burns and cuts, but not for insect bites.

(2) [　　　] Three hundred kinds of aloe are now used in medicine, food, and cosmetics.

(3) [　　　] Polysaccharide, the main ingredient of aloe vera, protects mucous membranes.

２．次の質問に対する答えとして最も適切なものを (A) 〜 (D) の中から選びましょう。

(1) Which family of plants does aloe belong to?

(A) The lily family

(B) The cactus family

(C) The banana family

(D) The fig family

(2) According to the passage, what are three ways aloe vera positively impacts health?

(A) It removes wrinkles and bags, promotes healthier blood circulation, and detoxifies.

(B) It makes people look younger, improves blood circulation, and increases bone density.

(C) It produces collagen, creates hyaluronic acid, and discharges bodily waste.

(D) It strengthens the immune system, prevents viral infection, and improves blood pressure.

(3) Why is Miyako-jima Island rich in coral limestone, alkaline soil, and minerals?

(A) The island is located in the subtropical zones.

(B) The ocean current brings a wide variety of minerals to this island.

(C) The coastal region of the island resembles the Mediterranean coasts of North Africa.

(D) The upheaval of coral reefs caused a mineral-rich landmass.

Grammar Points

五文型

1. 第1文型：SV→ 主語＋完全自動詞
2. 第2文型：SVC→ 主語＋不完全自動詞＋補語
   補語となるのは、名詞句・形容詞・前置詞句（例えばbe at home[気楽]など）
   動詞は典型的にはbe動詞であるが、次の動詞に注意（直後に形容詞がくる）
   →look（見える）、sound（聞こえる）、smell（匂う）、taste（味がする）、feel（感じる）
   触覚を表すfeel：This desk feels rough.（この机は触るとザラザラしている。）
3. 第3文型：SVO→ 主語＋完全他動詞＋目的語
4. 第4文型：SVOO→ 主語＋授与動詞＋間接目的語＋直接目的語
5. 第5文型：SVOC→ 主語＋不完全他動詞＋目的語＋補語
   補語となるのは、名詞句・形容詞・前置詞句（例えばput＋O＋in 〜の形）、および、原形不定詞（to doのtoのない形：使役動詞や知覚感覚動詞[seeやhearなど]のとき）

次の英文の ( ) 内に入る適切な語 (句) を (A)~(D) の中から選びましょう。

(1) Aloe is so effective in healing that some (　　　) it almost mystical.
　　(A) consider　　　(B) look　　　(C) regard　　　(D) seem

(2) The fact that aloe is mistakenly considered to belong to the cactus family is (　　　) to understand because of its appearance and texture.
　　(A) easy　　　(B) considerate　　　(C) important　　　(D) necessary

(3) Let us (　　　) one of the most well-known varieties of aloe.
　　(A) mention　　　(B) talk　　　(C) tell　　　(D) touch

(4) Though aloe might (　　　) bitter, it is rich in various kinds of nutrients.
　　(A) flavor　　　(B) flavor like　　　(C) taste　　　(D) taste like

(5) Some active ingredients found in aloe vera (　　　) effectively to treat burns.
　　(A) business　　　(B) job　　　(C) task　　　(D) work

Chapter 5 A Truly Bitter Medicinal Herb

❯ Composition Clues

次の英文の（　　　）内の語を並べ替えて、日本語訳に合う英文にしましょう。

(1) Aloe is (effective / greatly / in / so / the) improvement of our health that some may call it a cure-all.

アロエは我々の健康状態の改善にとても効果的なので万能薬と呼ぶ人がいます。

(　　　　　　　　　　　　　　　　　　　　　　　　　　　　　　　　)

(2) The medical benefits of some plants (antiquity / been / have / known / since) all over the world.

ある種の植物の医学的な効能は、世界中で太古より知られています。

(　　　　　　　　　　　　　　　　　　　　　　　　　　　　　　　　)

(3) (classification / in / its / regard / to), garlic belongs to the same lily family of plants as aloe.

分類に関していえば、大蒜 [にんにく] はアロエと同じユリ科に属しています。

(　　　　　　　　　　　　　　　　　　　　　　　　　　　　　　　　)

* 文頭に置かれる単語であっても小文字になっています

(4) The climate (in / of / parts / southern / the) the Arabian Peninsula is suitable for the growth of aloe.

アラビア半島南部の気候はアロエの成長に適しています。

(　　　　　　　　　　　　　　　　　　　　　　　　　　　　　　　　)

(5) Polysaccharide, the main ingredient of aloe vera, is (collagen / help / produce / said / to) and hyaluronic acid.

多糖体はアロエベラの主要成分であるが、コラーゲンとヒアルロン酸を生成するのに役立っていると言われています。

(　　　　　　　　　　　　　　　　　　　　　　　　　　　　　　　　)

35

Listening and Dictation

次の本文の要約文を聞いて、空所に英単語を書き入れましょう。その後、その単語を下の枠内から選び、その記号で答えましょう。

Only six or seven (1. _____) of 300 to 500 kinds of aloe are now used in (2. _____), foods, and cosmetics. Aloe vera is most (3. _____) because of its wide-ranging effectiveness. The word "aloe" comes from the Arabic word meaning "bitter," while the word "vera" is (4. _____) from the Latin word meaning "true."

The main (5. _____) of aloe vera is polysaccharide, which contributes to the protection of mucous membranes. It prevents (6. _____) infection, and can produce (7. _____) and hyaluronic acid. It also (8. _____) a type of detox while promoting good bacteria growth in the bowels. On top of this, aloe vera can help (9. _____) by promoting healthier blood circulation, even as it increases bone density. It is no (10. _____) to say that aloe vera can be considered a cure-all.

(a) collagen	(b) derived	(c) exaggeration	(d) ingredient	(e) medicine
(f) noteworthy	(g) out	(h) performs	(i) rejuvenate	(j) viral

科学よもやま話 5.　　ビタミンB12 とアロエ

　ビタミンB12は動物にしか含まれないものと考えられてきましたが、アロエベラには含まれているので、アロエは奇跡の植物と言われています。ビタミンB12は、葉酸と一緒になればスムーズに赤血球を作るので、造血に深く関わります。また、核酸・タンパク質の合成をはじめ、脂質や糖質の代謝に広く関わっています。

　ビタミンB12が不足すると、疲労・手足のしびれ・便秘・頭痛・めまい・動悸・消化不良・食欲不振・肝臓障害・脾臓障害・神経障害・悪性貧血・白血球や赤血球の減少などが起こる可能性があります。例えば、ビタミンB12が不足した赤血球は大きく変形してしまって、毛細血管に入れなくなり、血行不良の原因となります。すると、生命の源である酸素を体の隅々まで運ぶことが出来なくなります。

Chapter 5   A Truly Bitter Medicinal Herb

Talk and Discussion

次の 2 つのトピックでトークまたはディスカッションをしましょう。

1. What are some other healthy plants like aloe?

_____
_____

2. Do you think that herbal medicine such as Chinese kanpo is an effective way to treat certain medical conditions?

_____
_____

 Useful Expressions

(1) To give some further examples …. .
(2) Opinions differ, but I believe …. .
(3) As is often pointed out, …. .
(4) Though little is known about …, I would like to say …. .
(5) Though the general consensus is …, my view is that …. .

コミュニケーションのコツ 5. ＜主語を常に考える＞

「〜は不必要だ」と言いたいとします。これは、何を主語にするかによって、表現方法が異なってきます。例えば「それについて、心配は不要だ」を英語で言う場合、4種類の主語で表現できます。

(a) You don't need to worry about it.
(b) Worrying about it is not needed.
(c) It is unnecessary for you to worry about it.
(d) There is no need for you to worry about it.

(a)は人主語、(b)は物事主語、(c)はit主語、(d)はthere主語です。英語では、この4つの主語があり得るので、常に、この主語の4種類を意識し、同じ主語のパターンのみにしないことがコミュニケーションを充実させるコツと言えるでしょう。

Health

Chapter 6　The Healthiest Fruit?

キウイが一番健康によい果物か？

どんな食べ物が健康に良いのかが話題となることがあります。「少糖多果」（砂糖は少なく、果物は多く）という言葉があるぐらい果物は健康に良いのです。では、どんな果物がお勧めでしょうか？実はキウイがその候補のようです。この果物の秘密を探ってみましょう。

▶ Vocabulary Check

1〜7の単語の意味を (a) 〜 (g) から選びましょう。

1. exceed
2. outweigh
3. normal
4. consume
5. effective
6. derive
7. originate

(a) to use time, energy or things, and the like
(b) working in the way something is expected
(c) to be more than a certain amount or number
(d) to start in a particular situation
(e) to be more important or valuable than another
(f) usual, typical, or expected; not strange
(g) to come or develop from something else

Chapter 6 — The Healthiest Fruit?

Reading

With all the fruit available, it's sometimes hard to know which is best, and especially how much we should consume. According to Japanese authorities, the ideal daily intake of fruit is 200 grams. Some people may slightly exceed this recommended amount, but this doesn't necessarily mean they will gain weight and become fat. The benefits of fruits easily outweigh the cons. Eating fruit daily can protect us from disease, benefit the liver, and contribute to more beautiful skin.

One of the healthiest fruits is the kiwi fruit. Each kiwi is chock-full of nutrients. One kiwi fruit, which weighs about 100 grams, contains 100 milligrams of vitamin C, which is the recommended daily intake.

The suggested daily amount of dietary fiber is more than 21 grams for men, and more than 18 grams for women. One hundred grams of banana provides only 1.1 grams of dietary fiber. A single kiwi contains 2.6 grams. Therefore, adding two kiwi fruits a day to a normal diet easily reaches the recommended amount.

The amount of potassium that should be consumed daily is over 3,000 milligrams for men, and over 2,600 milligrams for women. One kiwi contains about 300 milligrams of potassium, amongst the highest of all fruits. This is more than twice the amount in grapefruits, and more than three times that in apples on a 100-gram basis. Even so, bananas still come out on top, with 360 milligrams of potassium. One major beneficial effect of potassium is the reduction and prevention of high blood pressure.

There are other nutrients found in relatively large amounts in kiwi fruits. These include vitamin K, known for its antioxidative effect; vitamin E, which is effective in blood coagulation; vitamin B6, which contributes to healthier skin and membranes; calcium, which is necessary for the growth of strong bones and teeth; magnesium, which is effective in preventing lifestyle-related diseases; phosphorus, needed for the healthy growth of bones and muscles; copper, which aids in the development of bones, liver, blood and the brain; and finally, folic acid, which is important in cell growth.

The word "kiwi" derives from the name of the national bird of New Zealand because the fruit and bird share a similar appearance. The name of the bird is said to have originated from the native New Zealanders, the Maori. It comes from the sound a male kiwi makes, a distinct "ki-wi."

Notes

cons 短所 / chock-full of ～ ～がぎっしり詰まって / dietary fiber 食物繊維 / potassium カリウム / antioxidative 抗酸化の / coagulation 凝固 / membrane 粘膜 / lifestyle-related disease 生活習慣病 / phosphorus 燐 (リン) / folic acid 葉酸

▶ Comprehension

１．次の文が本文の内容と一致する場合は T を、異なる場合は F を記入しましょう。

(1) [   ] If you eat more than the recommended amount of fruit, you will surely gain weight.

(2) [   ] You can get the recommended daily amount of vitamin C by eating one kiwi fruit.

(3) [   ] The name of the national bird of New Zealand comes from the shape of the kiwi fruit.

２．次の質問に対する答えとして最も適切なものを (A) ～ (D) の中から選びましょう。

(1) How much dietary fiber does 100 grams of banana provide?

(A) Over 21 grams

(B) More than 18 grams

(C) No more than 1.1 grams

(D) At least 2.6 grams

(2) How much potassium does one kiwi contain?

(A) Ten times the recommended daily amount of potassium

(B) Nearly one tenth of the recommended daily amount for men

(C) Less than one tenth of the recommended daily amount for women

(D) Three times the amount of potassium contained in all other fruit

(3) What kind of effect does vitamin E have on our body?

(A) It has an antioxidative effect.

(B) It assists with blood coagulation.

(C) It provides healthier skin and membranes.

(D) It prevents lifestyle-related diseases.

Grammar Points

受動態

be＋過去分詞の形
1. S（主語）V（動詞）O（目的語）⇒
   O be動詞 + V（動詞）の過去分詞形 by S

	過去分詞	現在分詞
be	受動態	進行形
have	完了形	×

2. 自動詞でもV（動詞）＋P（前置詞）の形が1つの動詞として使われる場合は、受動態が可能である。
   → The baby was looked after by an old woman.

3. 目的語が動詞の行為により影響を受けるほど受動態になりやすい。
   → I have many books. ⇒ × Many books are had by me.
     She ate the apple. ⇒ ○ The apple was eaten by her.

4. 後ろに付く前置詞により意味が異なることに注意する。
   → known for ～：～で知られている / known to ～：～に知られている
     known as ～：～として知られている / known by ～：～によって分かる
     ※A person is known by his or her friend.（友達を見ればその人が分かるものだ）

次の英文の( )内に入る適切な語(句)を (A)~(D) の中から選びましょう。

(1) The recommended daily amount of potassium to be (　　　) is more than 3,000 milligrams for men, and over 2,600 milligrams for women.
   (A) consume　　(B) consumed　　(C) consuming　　(D) consumption

(2) A wide variety of nutrients (　　　) in relatively large amounts in kiwi fruits.
   (A) are found　　(B) found　　(C) founding　　(D) to be founded

(3) Vitamin K, known (　　　) its antioxidative effect, is contained in large amounts in kiwi fruits.
   (A) as　　(B) by　　(C) for　　(D) to

(4) We can say that phosphorus is (　　　) for the healthy growth of bones and muscles.
   (A) necessity　　(B) need　　(C) needed　　(D) needs

(5) The word "kiwi" (　　　) come from the national bird of New Zealand.
   (A) is said that it has　　　　(B) is said to have
   (C) said to have　　　　(D) says to be

41

Composition Clues

次の英文の（　　）内の語を並べ替えて、日本語訳に合う英文にしましょう。

(1) An adequate intake of magnesium can (from / lifestyle-related / protect / us / diseases).
マグネシウムの適切な摂取は、我々を生活習慣病から守ってくれます。
(　　　　　　　　　　　　　　　　　　　　　　　　　　　　　　　　　)

(2) The (daily / dietary / intake / of / recommended) fiber is over 18 grams for women.
食物繊維の一日の推奨摂取量は女性の場合、18グラム以上です。
(　　　　　　　　　　　　　　　　　　　　　　　　　　　　　　　　　)

(3) Various kinds of nutrients are (amounts / contained / in / large / relatively) in kiwi fruits.
キウイには様々な種類の栄養素が比較的多く含まれています。
(　　　　　　　　　　　　　　　　　　　　　　　　　　　　　　　　　)

(4) The potassium found in one kiwi is (amount / more / than / the / twice) contained in grapefruits of the same weight.
キウイ1個のカリウム量は、同重量のグレープフルーツに含まれる量の2倍以上です。
(　　　　　　　　　　　　　　　　　　　　　　　　　　　　　　　　　)

(5) Calcium is said to (aid / growth / healthy / in / the) of bones and teeth.
カルシウムは骨や歯の健康的な成長を助けると言われています。
(　　　　　　　　　　　　　　　　　　　　　　　　　　　　　　　　　)

Chapter 6　The Healthiest Fruit?

▶ Listening and Dictation

次の本文の要約文を聞いて、空所に英単語を書き入れましょう。その後、その単語を下の枠内から選び、その記号で答えましょう。

　　　In general, fruit is good for health. The ideal daily (1.　　　　) of fruit is 200 grams. From the (2.　　　　) of nutritional science, the kiwi fruit may be the best. Kiwis are chock-full of (3.　　　　). For example, we can (4.　　　　) the recommended daily intake of vitamin C by eating one kiwi a day. One kiwi (5.　　　　) more than twice the amount of dietary fiber found in bananas of the same weight. It also contains more than (6.　　　　) times the amount of potassium in (7.　　　　) of the same weight.

　　　The kiwi is also (8.　　　　) in other nutrients like vitamin K, vitamin E, vitamin B6, calcium, magnesium, phosphorus, copper, and (9.　　　　) acid. All of these nutrients play a (10.　　　　) role in our health.

(a) apples	(b) contains	(c) folic	(d) intake	(e) meet
(f) nutrients	(g) rich	(h) significant	(i) three	(j) viewpoint

科学よもやま話 6.　果物の名前にはP系列の文字が入る？

　英語の果物の名前に、p系列の文字が入っています。例えば、pの文字は、apples（林檎）, pineapples（パイナップル）, peaches（桃）, pears（梨）, persimmons（柿）, grapes（ブドウ）, pomegranates（柘榴［ざくろ］）に見られます。また、pを濁音化したbが入っている果物は、bananas（バナナ）やstrawberries（苺）などがあります。

　一方、kiwiのように、他の文化から入った単語にはこのことが当てはまらないようです。他にメジャーな果物でP系列の文字が入っていない果物にorangeがあります。この言葉は元来、「よい香り」を意味するnarangaというサンスクリット語に由来し、この語がペルシャ語、アラビア語を経由してフランス語に入りました。不定冠詞が付いて、a narangaがan arangaと異分析され、anを除くarangaが英語に入ってorangeのようになったという説があるようです。

▶ Talk and Discussion

次の2つのトピックでトークまたはディスカッションをしましょう。

1. What do you do to stay healthy?
_____
_____

2. Name three fruits you like and how you like to eat them.
_____
_____

Useful Expressions

(1) What I do to keep my health is …. .
(2) There is considerable doubt about …. .
(3) It is a demonstrable truth, but I want to say …. .
(4) Whether this is true or not, I would like to say …. .
(5) This is not the end of the story. I have to say …. .

コミュニケーションのコツ 6.　〈使えるディスカッション展開表現〉

(1) This is part and parcel of my theory.（これが私の理論の骨子です）
(2) Here lies the kernel of the matter.（要点はここにあります）
(3) The long and short of my hypothesis is this.（私の仮説の要点はこうです）
(4) The point I would like to show here is this.（ここで示したいポイントはこれです）
(5) Let me analyze the discussion of the problem.
　　（その問題に関する議論を分析しましょう）
(6) With these ideas in mind, observe the following example.
　　（これらの考えを踏まえて、次の例を観察しましょう）
　　注：(6)のwith以下とobserve以下にいろいろなものを入れることができるので、応用
　　　　表現が多い。
　　→ With these definitions in mind, observe the following view.
　　　（これらの定義を踏まえて、次の見解を見てみましょう）
　　　 With these problems in mind, observe the following plan.
　　　（これらの問題を踏まえて、次の計画を見てみましょう）

Technology

Chapter 7
Life-changing Smart Devices

スマートマットレスと睡眠改善

現代は、時計やカード、家電や眼鏡に至るまで、インターネットを通して繋がる時代です。どんなスマートデバイスが我々の生活に現れてくるのかが楽しみですが、ここでは、健康的な睡眠をサポートしてくれるスマートマットレスについて取り上げます。

▶ Vocabulary Check

1～7の単語の意味を (a)～(g) から選びましょう。

1. efficient
2. connect
3. define
4. unmanned
5. embed
6. calculate
7. satisfactory

(a) good enough for a particular need or purpose
(b) to explain the meaning of a specific word or idea
(c) to put something firmly or deeply into something else
(d) to join two or more things together
(e) to find out the number or amount of something
(f) working well without wasting time, money or energy
(g) with no people in an aircraft, spaceship, or similar vessel

▶ Reading

🎧 1-47〜54

A smart device is a generic name for information-processing equipment beyond the framework of personal computers, mainframes, or workstations. Mainframes are large-scale computers used for the information systems in large organizations. Workstations, on the other hand, are highly efficient office computers used for business purposes. A smart
5 device is something else entirely, in form and function.

Smart devices are a product of IoT technology, which connects various things through the Internet. IoT stands for Internet of Things, which means the Internet connecting things in general. This is in contrast to the typical connections between computers that had previously defined the Internet.
10 Smart devices include smartwatches, smart cards, smart home electric appliances, and smart glasses. Drones can also sometimes be classified as a form of smart device. A drone is an unmanned aircraft flown by remote control, which has a number of practical uses.

An example of an eclectic smart device would be the smart mattress. This novel mattress is characterized by a special sensor embedded in it. The sensor can measure sleeping hours
15 and conditions by monitoring a person's movements and sounds as they sleep.

It is the sleep score that the sleepers can check through this sensor. The score indicates how to improve sleep. It is calculated based on the following six items: sleeping hours, sleeping efficiency, the time needed to fall sleep, the number of times a sleeper awakes during the night, awakening conditions in the morning, and deep sleep. People can receive
20 greater insight into their sleep habits because of this.

It seems that this device is satisfactory in itself; however, its full power is realized when it is connected to other electronics. Some smart mattresses can be connected with air conditioners or lighting, for example. The air conditioner can automatically control the temperatures and air direction during sleep. Also, automatically adjusting the lighting can
25 make it possible for people to wake up more naturally by making the room gradually brighter.

It is hoped that smart mattresses will help improve sleep for those who can't sleep soundly, such as people suffering from insomnia.

In the near future, we will be able to connect all equipment, including furniture and
30 electrical appliances, through the Internet. It is hard to imagine what kind of changes are in store for us in this brave new world of constant connectivity.

Notes •••

mainframe メインフレーム [汎用の大型コンピュータ] / workstation ワークステーション [事務処理な どに特化した業務用の高性能なコンピュータ] / IoT モノのインターネット [Internet of Things の略] / smart home electric appliances スマート家電 / eclectic 折衷的な / insomnia 不眠症 / brave new world 素 晴らしき新世界、未来社会

46

Chapter 7 Life-changing Smart Devices

⊙ Comprehension

１．次の文が本文の内容と一致する場合は T を、異なる場合は F を記入しましょう。

(1) [   ] Typical examples of smart devices include mainframes and workstations.

(2) [   ] A smart device connects various kinds of things through the Internet.

(3) [   ] A special sensor is embedded in a certain smart home electric appliance.

２．次の質問に対する答えとして最も適切なものを (A) ～ (D) の中から選びましょう。

(1) What is NOT included in the items that the sleep score is based on?

    (A) The period of time spent sleeping

    (B) The time one needs to fall sleep

    (C) How often one wakes up during the night

    (D) How often one turns over in bed

(2) What can be done if the smart mattress is connected with an air conditioner?

    (A) It can control the direction of the air flow.

    (B) It can monitor the sleeper's movements during the night.

    (C) It can make the room gradually brighter.

    (D) It can heat up the mattress.

(3) According to the passage, what kind of people will a smart mattress help most?

    (A) People who sleep too much and cannot get up early

    (B) People who have trouble sleeping and suffer from lack of sleep

    (C) People having trouble breathing while sleeping

    (D) People who are bothered by bright lights at night

Grammar Points

itの用法

1. 人称代名詞：人以外の物で単数の物を受ける。
2. 非人称のit：天候・時間・距離・寒暖・明暗・状況などを表す。
   → make it feel as if … (…と感じさせる)
3. 仮主語・仮目的語のit：It is important to do.（仮主語）
   　　　　　　　　　　 I make it a rule to do…．（仮目的語）
   注：難易構文は、以下の書き換えが可能。
   　　It is hard to know what will happen. =What will happen is hard to know.
4. 強調構文のit：It is John that loves Mary.（メアリーを愛しているのはジョンだ。）

次の英文の（　）内に入る適切な語(句)を (A)~(D) の中から選びましょう。

(1) One characteristic of the smart mattress is a special sensor embedded in (　　　).
　　(A) it　　　　　(B) one　　　　　(C) them　　　　　(D) which

(2) It is sleeping efficiency (　　　) we have to check for better sleep.
　　(A) for　　　　(B) that　　　　　(C) what　　　　　(D) where

(3) (　　　) seems that in the near future, we will be able to connect most electronics to the Internet.
　　(A) It　　　　 (B) There　　　　(C) We　　　　　　(D) What

(4) The control of the air direction from an air conditioner can (　　　) possible for us to sleep soundly.
　　(A) has it　　　(B) has us　　　　(C) make it　　　　(D) make us

(5) The rapid progress of science and technology makes (　　　) hard to imagine what kind of changes are in store for us.
　　(A) how　　　　(B) it　　　　　　(C) us　　　　　　(D) very

Chapter 7　Life-changing Smart Devices

❯ Composition Clues

次の英文の（　　　　）内の語を並べ替えて、日本語訳に合う英文にしましょう。

(1) The connections between computers and IoT (are / contrast / in / those / to) between computers through the ordinary Internet.
IoT に見られるコンピュータと物との接続は従来のインターネットに見られるコンピュータ同士の接続と対照的です。
(　　　　　　　　　　　　　　　　　　　　　　　　　　　　　　　　)

(2) A transportation IC card like ICOCA (a / as / classified / form / is) of smart card.
ICOCA のような交通系 IC カードはスマートカードの一形態として分類されます。
(　　　　　　　　　　　　　　　　　　　　　　　　　　　　　　　　)

(3) By analyzing the sleep score, we can receive (a / insight / into / more / profound) our sleep habits.
睡眠スコアを分析することにより、我々は睡眠習慣についてもっと深く理解することができます。
(　　　　　　　　　　　　　　　　　　　　　　　　　　　　　　　　)

(4) If the smart (air / are / connected / mattresses / to) conditioners or lighting, their full power is realized.
もしスマートマットレスがエアコンや照明器具と接続すれば、その能力が最大に発揮されます。
(　　　　　　　　　　　　　　　　　　　　　　　　　　　　　　　　)

(5) (hoped / is / it / modern / that) people's sleep habits will be improved by using smart mattresses.
そのスマートマットレスを利用して、現代人の睡眠習慣が改善されることが望まれています。
(　　　　　　　　　　　　　　　　　　　　　　　　　　　　　　　　)
＊文頭に置かれる単語であっても小文字になっています

49

Listening and Dictation

次の本文の要約文を聞いて、空所に英単語を書き入れましょう。その後、その単語を下の枠内から選び、その記号で答えましょう。

A smart device is (1. _____) different from ordinary information-processing equipment such as personal computers, mainframes, or workstations. An IT product (2. _____) various things through the Internet. (3. _____) examples include smartwatches, smart cards, smart home electric appliances, and smart glasses.

A smart mattress, in which a special sensor is (4. _____), helps people improve their sleep habits. Since the sensor can (5. _____) a sleep score, people having trouble sleeping can check six (6. _____) related to sleep, so that they can hopefully sleep more (7. _____). When this smart device is connected to other home electric appliances, its full power is (8. _____).

IT technology and its related products will continue to be an (9. _____) part of our future as engineers continue to find (10. _____) ways to connect us to the Internet.

| (a) categories | (b) connects | (c) embedded | (d) entirely | (e) exciting |
| (f) indicate | (g) innovative | (h) realized | (i) soundly | (j) typical |

科学よもやま話 7.　　スマートテレビ

スマートテレビはインターネットに接続することでインターネット上の多様なコンテンツを視聴できる機能を備えています。機能がスマホに共通するので、スマホの機能が内蔵されたテレビ、言わば、スマホのテレビ版です。

通常のテレビのように一方的に番組を提供し、チャンネルで選ぶという方式ではなく、視聴者が自らのタイミングで番組を見たり、双方向での参加が可能な仕組みがありますが、これは、現代のトレンドに合致しています。

スマートテレビは通例、リモコンで操作しますが、リモコンで音声入力ができる製品も増えていて、話しかけるだけで検索を行うことができ、好きな番組を自由に視聴することができます。

Chapter 7　Life-changing Smart Devices

▶ Talk and Discussion

次の２つのトピックでトークまたはディスカッションをしましょう。

1. What kind of smart device do you think is most convenient?

_____
_____

2. How will technology change in the next 20 years? How about in the next 100 years?

_____
_____

Useful Expressions

(1) What I think is very convenient is …. .
(2) There is no need for you to worry about …. .
(3) There is no telling …. .
(4) The long and short of it is that …. .
(5) We can safely say that …. .

コミュニケーションのコツ 7.　＜ディベートの手法を活かす＞

「証拠」（Data）とは「主張」（Claim）を支えるデータ（資料や数的情報）ですが、「論拠」（Warrant）とは証拠の権威付けや一般常識であり、これも主張を支えます。証拠のデータの出所がその研究の権威者であれば論拠となります。

一般に、証拠は新情報で、論拠は旧情報であることが多いもので、新情報はbecause（［あなたは知らないと思うが］～だから）を用い、旧情報はsince（［あなたも知っているように］～だから）を用いることになるのが普通です。

主張を論破するには、証拠が不完全または不適切であること、論拠が不適切または無意味であること、或いは、主張と証拠や論拠の結び付け（reasoning）が非論理的（illogical）であることを示すとよいでしょう。

Technology

Chapter 8: The Rise of Generative AI

生成 AI はどこまで進化するか？

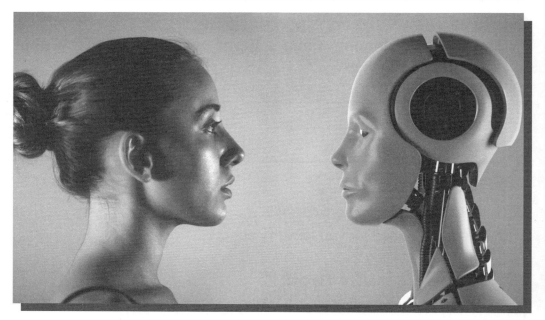

生成 AI の ChatGPT が話題となって久しいですが、この生成 AI と従来の AI とはどう違うのでしょうか。最近の生成 AI は、「想像力」や「創造力」という能力まで持つようになりました。ここでは、生成 AI について掘り下げて、将来の更なる可能性を探ります。

▶ Vocabulary Check

1 〜 7 の単語の意味を (a) 〜 (g) から選びましょう。

1. characterize
2. generate
3. precision
4. specialize
5. noteworthy
6. handle
7. detach

(a) to separate someone or something from a situation
(b) interesting or important enough to deserve your attention
(c) the quality of being very exact or correct
(d) to deal with a situation or problem by behaving in a particular way
(e) to produce or bring about something
(f) to be typical of a thing, a person, or a place
(g) to limit most of your study or business to a particular subject or activity

Chapter 8 The Future Development of Generative AI

Recently, there has been a lot of hype surrounding the popularity and usefulness of artificial intelligence, especially generative AI. Generative AI can quickly produce original text and images. It is further characterized by its ability to generate new data based on rapid learning. It therefore develops in the same way as a human mind does, but with some major caveats.

The major difference between generative AI and conventional AI is that the former can generate texts or images more rapidly, emphasizing precision and creativity. Therefore, generative AI can do jobs which were once possible only by humans.

Services used by generative AI include ChatGPT, Stable Diffusion, and Gemini. ChatGPT, which was developed by OpenAI, Inc., specializes in creating text. This AI is constantly being updated for efficiency. Its performance utilizing multiple languages interchangeably is incredible, with its speed being especially noteworthy. Stable Diffusion focuses on generating images. A user simply has to enter prompts, which the AI uses to quickly produce an image. Finally, Gemini is a generative AI service developed by Google, which is characterized by multimodal technology. This AI can simultaneously handle a variety of data, such as text, images, and animation.

Like most new technology, generative AI has advantages and disadvantages. On the plus side, it increases work efficiency, offers almost unlimited variety in its creations, and can be more innovative than humans. On the negative side, there is the risk of AI being abused to destabilize societies through mimicry or the spreading of disinformation. AI may also take jobs from humans. Lastly, AI commonly provides false answers, or "hallucinations," to queries.

The problem of AI taking away jobs from humans is serious. Generative AI can handle professional or creative tasks that, until now, could never be done by machines. For example, interpreters may lose work due to the speed and accuracy of AI in translating languages.

Regarding hallucinations, AI can sometimes not distinguish between accurate and false information, causing it to draw its own conclusions based on faulty data. Judging whether something is true or not is often hard for humans. It can be even harder for AI.

The ubiquitousness of AI may pose other challenges. Lonely people, especially teens, may establish romantic relationships with AI programs, resulting in people becoming detached from reality. Someone who continually converses with AI instead of humans may develop poor social skills and eventually have trouble socializing with others.

Notes

hype 誇大広告 / caveat 注意、警告 / Stable Diffusion Stability AI 社が開発した 画像生成 AI / Gemini Google が開発したマルチモーダル生成 AI / enter prompts プロンプトを入力する / multimodal マルチモードの [文字・音声・画像・動画など同時に作成できる] / simultaneously 同時に / destabilize 不安定にする / mimicry 真似 / disinformation 偽情報 / hallucinations 幻覚、妄想 / query (不審を含んだ) 質問 / ubiquitousness 偏在性 [至る所にあること]

❯ Comprehension

1. 次の文が本文の内容と一致する場合は T を、異なる場合は F を記入しましょう。

(1) [   ] Features of generative AI include its ability to make new data based on rapid learning.

(2) [   ] Generative AI still cannot do many kinds of jobs that are possible only by humans.

(3) [   ] ChatGPT is a service using generative AI, but Gemini is not.

2. 次の質問に対する答えとして最も適切なものを (A) ～ (D) の中から選びましょう。

(1) What is Stable Diffusion used for?

(A) For the generation of texts

(B) For the printing of photographs

(C) For the creation of images

(D) None of the above

(2) What can be done through a service based on multimodal technology?

(A) Connect different computers very quickly

(B) Be able to deal with a variety of data at the same time

(C) Get rid of serious disadvantages simultaneously

(D) Establish romantic relationships with AI programs

(3) Which is one of the most serious disadvantages of generative AI?

(A) The possibility of AI dominating humans in the near future

(B) The fact that AI may spread information that could cause trouble

(C) The danger that AI could give too many tasks to humans

(D) The risk of AI being used to translate ancient languages

Chapter 8　The Future Development of Generative AI

▶ Grammar Points

時制

1. 時制には、過去・現在・未来という基本三時制がある。
   過去は「過去形」、現在は「現在形」、未来は「will＋動詞の原形」で表せる。
2. 上記の三時制それぞれに、(1)完了形と(2)進行形と(3)完了進行形の形がある。

	(1)完了形	(2)進行形	(3)完了進行形
過去	had done	was/were doing	had been doing
現在	have/has done	is/am/are doing	have/has been doing
未来	will have done	will be doing	will have been doing

3. 各時制と相性のよい副詞が存在する。
   → ・過去をはっきり表す副詞（句・節）は過去時制と共に用いられる。
   ・already（完了の意味）、three times（経験の意味）、since ～（～以来：継続の意味）は、完了形と共に用いられる。
   ・recentlyやin recent yearsは過去形または現在完了形と共に用いられる。

次の英文の（　）内に入る適切な語（句）を (A)~(D) の中から選びましょう。

(1) There (　　) a lot of discussion about the possibility of AI dominating humans in recent years.
　　(A) had been　　(B) has been　　(C) is　　(D) will be

(2) The newest version of ChatGPT (　　) released by OpenAI, Inc., last month.
　　(A) has been　　(B) is　　(C) was　　(D) will be

(3) Generative AI increases work efficiency and (　　) almost unlimited variety in its creations.
　　(A) offer　　(B) offered　　(C) offering　　(D) offers

(4) Generative AI can deal with creative tasks that could never (　　) by ordinary computers.
　　(A) have done　　(B) have been done　　(C) had been doing　　(D) able to do

(5) The situation where a lonely person establishes romantic relationships with AI programs (　　) in them becoming detached from reality.
　　(A) could result　　(B) have resulted　　(C) resulting　　(D) to result

55

▶ Composition Clues

次の英文の（　　　）内の語を並べ替えて、日本語訳に合う英文にしましょう。

(1) Generative AI (by / capability / characterized / is / its) of generating texts or images more rapidly than conventional AI.
生成 AI の特徴に、従来の AI よりテキストや画像を速く生成する能力があります。
(　　　　　　　　　　　　　　　　　　　　　　　　　　　　　　　　　　　）

(2) Generative AI (capable / is / making / of / texts) or images a lot more precisely and creatively than conventional AI .
生成 AI は従来の AI より、より正確に、より創造力を駆使して、テキストや画像を作成する能力があります。
(　　　　　　　　　　　　　　　　　　　　　　　　　　　　　　　　　　　）

(3) Gemini (focuses / multimodal / on / primarily / technology), under which a variety of data is handled.
Gemini は主に、様々なデータが扱われるマルチモードの技術に焦点を当てています。
(　　　　　　　　　　　　　　　　　　　　　　　　　　　　　　　　　　　）

(4) In the near future, English teachers in Japan may (due / finding / have / trouble / work) to the invention of a convenient device which accurately interprets between English and Japanese.
近い将来、日本の英語教師は、英日間を正確に通訳する便利な機器の発明のため、仕事を探すのに苦労するかもしれません。
(　　　　　　　　　　　　　　　　　　　　　　　　　　　　　　　　　　　）

(5) Modern-day people tend to (a / devote / lot / of / their) time to using smartphones whenever they have the chance.
現代に生きる人たちは、暇さえあればスマホを使うということに多くの時間を捧げる傾向にあります。
(　　　　　　　　　　　　　　　　　　　　　　　　　　　　　　　　　　　）

56

Chapter 8　The Future Development of Generative AI

Listening and Dictation

 1-63

次の本文の要約文を聞いて、空所に英単語を書き入れましょう。その後、その単語を下の枠内から選び、その記号で答えましょう。

　　　Recently, generative AI is the (1.　　　　　) of the town. It is characterized by its ability to quickly produce original text and images. Generative AI can also (2.　　　　) in doing jobs which were once possible only by humans. Services (3.　　　　) by generative AI include ChatGPT, Stable Diffusion, and Gemini. Generally speaking, everything has merits and (4.　　　　). Generative AI is no (5.　　　　).

　　　There are a few positive (6.　　　　) of generative AI. It can help increase work efficiency. It offers an almost unlimited (7.　　　　) in its creations. It's also innovative in areas where humans may have difficulty. On the other hand, there are three major (8.　　　　). There's the risk of AI being (9.　　　　). There's also the danger of AI taking jobs from humans. Finally, there's the possibility of AI providing false answers to (10.　　　　).

(a) abused	(b) assist	(c) demerits	(d) drawbacks	(e) exception
(f) features	(g) provided	(h) queries	(i) talk	(j) variety

科学よもやま話 8.　GEMINI の凄さと AI 依存

　GEMINIは、創造力の高い仕事ができます。例えば、子どもが描いた、一見拙い絵に感動的な話を添えることができます。また、夏の暑い時期に、楽しい旅行プランを提案してくれます。複雑な創造的作業を速く行うことができる優れモノと言えるでしょう。

　人間がそれに依存しすぎると、人間の側の創造力が失われるだけでなく、本来人間らしさの象徴である「自分自身でしっかりと考えること」と「人とのコミュニケーションを楽しむこと」の2つの重要な人間的能力の涵養に悪影響を与える可能性があります。AIをうまく使いこなす（AIに使われてしまうのではなく、つまり、AI依存にならずに）ことが大切と言えるでしょう。

▶ Talk and Discussion

次の2つのトピックでトークまたはディスカッションをしましょう。

1. How do you want to make the best use of AI?

___

2. Do you think AI will dominate humans in the future?

___

Useful Expressions

(1) Let me tell you how I use …. .

(2) Let me give you one example. It is …. .

(3) To be more exact, I have to say …. .

(4) It is important, but even more important is the fact that …. .

(5) What you say and what I say are two different things. I just want to say …. .

コミュニケーションのコツ 8. ＜ディスカッションの始めと終わりの表現＞

(1) 始めの表現

It is a great pleasure to be given the opportunity to speak in front of you.
I am very happy to get the opportunity to give my own opinion today.
I am Taro Yamada, a student in the Department of Technology, Englight University.
I am Hanako Tanaka, majoring in history in the Department of Social Studies.

(2) 終わりの表現

That's all.
That's what I wanted to talk about today.
That's all (that) I wanted to talk about today.
I really enjoyed talking with you.
I think we were able to bring the discussion to a successful conclusion.
Thank you very much for listening to my opinion.
Thank you for your attention.

Technology

Chapter 9: What Is Quantum Computing?

量子コンピュータが世界を変える？

最先端の科学に量子力学がありますが、この科学を応用したコンピュータである量子コンピュータの世界を垣間見ましょう。これまでのコンピュータとどこが違うのでしょうか。少し難解かもしれない量子力学の「重ね合わせ」の世界にも科学のメスを入れます。

Vocabulary Check

1〜7の単語の意味を (a)〜(g) から選びましょう。

1. matter
2. enhance
3. conventional
4. measure
5. probability
6. employ
7. simultaneously

(a) the level of possibility of something happening or being true
(b) to be important or to have an effect on what happens
(c) to find the size, length, or amount of something
(d) to improve the amount, quality, or strength of something
(e) to use something for a particular purpose
(f) at the same time
(g) traditional and ordinary

In the realm of computers, size matters. Computer performance has been enhanced dramatically due to the development and miniaturization of semiconductor technology. If the circuits of a semiconductor are made smaller, operation speeds increase. Moreover, power consumption is also reduced. Therefore, we can say that semiconductor minimization is one of the keys to the advancement of computer technology.

The application of quantum computing to present IT technology will greatly contribute to the further development of computers. Quantum computing refers to the technology which uses principles related to quantum mechanics. This leads to solutions to complicated problems that cannot be dealt with by conventional computers.

Quantum mechanics is a field of science which deals with the laws of physics that apply to physical objects smaller than atoms. To be more specific, quantum mechanics attempts to explain the behavior of very small particles. The goal is to understand phenomena that can't be explained by classical physics alone. This makes quantum mechanics one of the two great fields of modern physics, the other being Einstein's theory of relativity.

Generally speaking, quanta include electrons, protons, and neutrons. However, protons and neutrons consist of smaller elementary particles called quarks. There are six kinds of quarks forming three generations. There's the first generation of up and down quarks. Next, there's the second generation of charm and strange quarks. Finally, the third generation consists of top and bottom quarks. A proton is composed of two up quarks and one down quark. A neutron is made up of two down quarks and one up quark.

As is often mentioned, quanta are characterized by the phenomenon of superposition. Superposition refers to the same particle existing in multiple states simultaneously. In short, until location, momentum, and energy can be measured, the multiple states exist in terms of probability only.

If the superposition principle in quantum mechanics is employed in the world of computer technology, processing capacity will be enhanced enormously. This will lead to the development of quantum computers. In conventional computers, a bit exists in the state of 0 or 1. In quantum computers, a quantum bit can hold the middle area between 0 and 1, and even more than two states at the same time. As a result, quantum computers can process several computing tasks simultaneously. Comparatively, conventional computers are limited in how many tasks they can perform at once.

Quantum computers are now under development as the cutting edge in the future of computing. It is hoped that in the near future, quantum computers can instantly solve some of the most complex problems that have stumped humanity for generations.

Chapter 9　What Is Quantum Computing?

Notes •

realm 領域 / miniaturization 小型化 / quantum computing 量子コンピューティング [量子力学を利用し
て複雑な問題を素早く解く技術] / quantum mechanics 量子力学 / classical physics 古典物理学 /
Einstein's theory of relativity アインシュタインの相対性理論 / quanta quantum の複数形。 量子 /
electron 電子 / proton 陽子 / neutron 中性子 / quark 陽子や中性子といった粒子を構成する基本的な粒子。
物質の最も基本的な構成要素の一つ。 / up and down quarks アップクォークとダウンクォーク / charm
and strange quarks チャームクォークとストレンジクォーク / top and bottom quarks トップクォークと
ボトムクォーク / superposition 重ね合わせ / momentum 運動量 / cutting edge 最前線 / stump 悩ませる

● Comprehension

1．次の文が本文の内容と一致する場合は T を、異なる場合は F を記入しましょう。

(1) [　　　] If the circuits of a semiconductor are made smaller, power consumption decreases.

(2) [　　　] Quantum computing is technology that uses the principles of the theory of
relativity.

(3) [　　　] The word "quanta" refers to very small particles like quarks, but not to electrons or
protons.

2．次の質問に対する答えとして最も適切なものを (A) 〜 (D) の中から選びましょう。

(1) How can we explain quantum mechanics?

(A) It is the field of science dealing with semiconductor minimization.

(B) Its application to present IT technology is unlikely to lead to the development of computers.

(C) It aims at understanding phenomena which cannot be fully explained by classical physics.

(D) It fundamentally deals with six kinds of quarks, and nothing else.

(2) What are the names of the second-generation quarks?

(A) Up and down quarks

(B) Charm and strange quarks

(C) Top and bottom quarks

(D) Big and small quarks

(3) What is the correct description of superposition?

(A) A single particle exists in multiple states at the same time.

(B) After we measure the momentum of a particle, its multiple states exist.

(C) A bit exists in the state of either 0 or 1, not in the middle area between 0 and 1.

(D) It describes the recent advances in computing speeds.

61

Grammar Points

自動詞と他動詞

1. 自動詞は目的語をとらない動詞、他動詞は目的語をとる動詞
   (1) 自動詞と間違えやすい動詞：attend（に出席する）、reach（に到着する）marry（と結婚する）、mention（について触れる）、discuss（について議論する）handle（を扱う）[×handle with]、tackle（に対処する）[×tackle with]
   (2) 他動詞と間違えやすい動詞：reply（答える [+to]）、apologize（謝る [to人for事]）object to ～（～に反対する）/ 注 oppose ～（～に反対する）[こちらは他動詞]
2. 自動詞と他動詞の両方を兼ねる動詞も多いが、意味が異なるものに注意する。
   →talk with 人（人と話す）、talk 人 into doing ～（人を説得して～させる）
3. 基本的な動詞は名詞と同形である。
   →swim（泳ぐ）/ 注 Let's have a swim.（ひと泳ぎしよう。）

次の英文の（　）内に入る適切な語（句）を (A)~(D) の中から選びましょう。

(1) In the field of IT technology, efficiency (　　　　).

　　(A) matters　　　　(B) objects　　　　(C) substances　　　　(D) things

(2) Quantum mechanics tackles the laws of physics that (　　　) to physical objects smaller than atoms.

　　(A) applies　　　　(B) apply　　　　(C) are applying　　　　(D) is applied

(3) A neutron (　　　) of two down quarks and one up quark.

　　(A) comprises　　　(B) constitutes　　　(C) is composed　　　(D) is consisted

(4) As is often (　　　), superposition is very hard to understand, and even harder to explain convincingly.

　　(A) mentioned　　(B) mentioned about　　(C) mentioning　　(D) mentioning about

(5) It is expected that quantum computers capable of (　　　) several computing tasks at the same time will exist in the future.

　　(A) being processed　　　　　　(B) having processed
　　(C) process　　　　　　　　　　(D) processing

Chapter 9 What Is Quantum Computing?

❯ Composition Clues

次の英文の （　　　） 内の語を並べ替えて、日本語訳に合う英文にしましょう。

(1) The active (application / IT / of / technology / to) Japan's university education will lead to greater efficiency in producing talented students.

IT 技術を日本の大学教育に積極的に適用していけば、能力のある学生の排出が一層効率的なものになるでしょう。

(　　　　　　　　　　　　　　　　　　　　　　　　　　　　　　　　　　　　)

(2) One of the two major principles of quantum mechanics is superposition, (being / entanglement / other / quantum / the).

量子力学の二大原理の一つは重ね合わせです。もう一つは量子もつれです。

(　　　　　　　　　　　　　　　　　　　　　　　　　　　　　　　　　　　　)

(3) A proton (made / is / of / up / two) up quarks and one down quark.

陽子は二つのアップクォークと一つのダウンクォークから成っています。

(　　　　　　　　　　　　　　　　　　　　　　　　　　　　　　　　　　　　)

(4) Traditional Japanese-style cell phones are (how / in / limited / many / tasks) they can perform at a time.

ガラ携は一度にどれくらいの仕事をこなせるかについて限界があります。

(　　　　　　　　　　　　　　　　　　　　　　　　　　　　　　　　　　　　)

(5) Nanotechnology (as / cutting / edge / of / the) sustainable agriculture plays a very important role in present society.

持続可能な農業の最前線としてのナノテクノロジーは、現代社会において重要な役割を担っています。

(　　　　　　　　　　　　　　　　　　　　　　　　　　　　　　　　　　　　)

63

Listening and Dictation

次の本文の要約文を聞いて、空所に英単語を書き入れましょう。その後、その単語を下の枠内から選び、その記号で答えましょう。

The application of quantum computing to present IT technology will (1.) lead to the (2.) development of computers. Quantum computing is based on technology which uses quantum mechanics-related principles. Quantum mechanics (3.) with the laws of physics that apply to very small (4.), even smaller than atoms. Quantum mechanics is one of the two great areas of physics, the other being Einstein's theory of relativity.

Superposition is one of the major (5.) in quantum mechanics. It refers to the (6.) existence of two different states: particles and waves. The two states exist at the same time in terms of (7.). Quantum computers (8.) principles of quantum mechanics are now under development. It is hoped that the extra (9.) power this provides will help solve very difficult problems (10.) quickly.

| (a) computational | (b) deals | (c) employing | (d) extremely | (e) further |
| (f) particles | (g) phenomena | (h) probability | (i) simultaneous | (j) surely |

科学よもやま話 9.　量子もつれとは？

「量子もつれ」(quantum entanglement)は興味深い現象です。例えば、2つの相関が強い玉が混然一体（赤と青）となっているが、それらを1光年離し、1つを赤と観測した瞬間にもう一方が青になるというような現象です。この赤い玉から、その情報を伝えると1年かかるところ、これが瞬時に起こるのです。

量子もつれの問題は、もはや時間の概念がないと言えるので、「量子の世界では「時空」が、般若心経で説き明かしている「空」である」と考えられます。同時に、意識の世界も時空を超えます。だからこそ、何光年も先の宇宙に想いを馳せる（＝意識を飛ばす）ことが可能なのです。物質世界の量子と精神世界の意識が「空」を通してリンクしているのは興味深いことです。

Chapter 9 What Is Quantum Computing?

▶ Talk and Discussion

次の 2 つのトピックでトークまたはディスカッションをしましょう。

1. What do you use computers for?

_____

_____

· ·

2. How do you think quantum computers will change the world?

_____

_____

Useful Expressions

(1) When it comes to .... , my preference is .... .

(2) What you have to bear in mind is .... .

(3) The thing is that .... . [=The point is that .... .]

(4) The opinion may differ from person to person, but I think .... .

(5) I kind of feel that .... .

コミュニケーションのコツ 9. ＜会話上手は聞き上手（相手の考えを引き出す表現）＞

Would you tell me what you think about the matter?
（その件について思うことを述べてください。）

Do you agree or disagree with his opinion?
（彼の意見に賛成ですか、反対ですか？）

Tell me what you know about it.
（それについて知っていることを教えてください。）

I hope you will give us more detailed information about it.
（そのことについて、もう少し詳しく教えていただけますか。）

I don't quite understand what you are talking about; would you be more specific?
（おっしゃっていることがよく分かりません。もう少し具体的にお願いできますか？）

65

Animals

Chapter 10
What if Cockroaches Were Extinct?

ゴキブリは本当に害虫か？

人間に嫌われている生物の代表はゴキブリと言えるでしょう。ゴキブリについて深く学べば、この昆虫が必ずしも害虫とは言えない面もあるのが分かります。その身体能力の凄さを感じつつ、ゴキブリのことを見直す機会となるかもしれません。

Vocabulary Check

1〜7の単語の意味を (a)〜(g) から選びましょう。

1. fossil
2. nuisance
3. virtually
4. frequent
5. consume
6. species
7. eradicate

(a) to use fuel, energy, time, or a product
(b) almost entirely or nearly
(c) to be in or visit a particular place often
(d) one that is harmful or annoying
(e) to eliminate or destroy completely
(f) an ancient organism preserved in rock or other materials
(g) different types of living organisms

Chapter 10 What if Cockroaches Were Extinct?

 Reading 1-72～77

　The most hated insect on Earth is probably the cockroach. Cockroaches, sometimes called living fossils, have existed for 300 million years, long before humans appeared on the planet. Though they are a nuisance, it can be said that humans are intruding on the cockroaches' territory, and not the other way around.

5　In their search for food, cockroaches will attempt to enter virtually any place. Their flat bodies allow them to squeeze through gaps as small as one or two millimeters. Typically, cockroaches enter homes through drains, vents, and air conditioning pipes. This is where the problem lies. Since they frequent unclean places full of germs, they carry bacteria such as shigella, salmonella, and vibrio cholerae on their bodies. When they feast on our food,
10　these bacteria can transfer to what we eat, posing a health risk to us.

　The resilience of cockroaches is quite incredible. A person may claim that their home is so clean that cockroaches cannot find any food, but this is far from the case. It is said that humans lose 50 to 100 hairs a day, and it is nearly impossible to clean all of them off the floor or furniture. Cockroaches can, and will, consume human hair if nothing else is
15　available. Cockroaches also consume grease. Even small splatters of grease from a frying pan to a counter or wall can become their food. Moreover, cockroaches can survive for extended periods of time on a diet of water alone. A single drop of water can sustain one roach for three days.

　Not all cockroaches are pests. There are about 4,000 species of cockroaches in the world
20　and around 60 species in Japan. Most of them play a role as decomposers in forests. For instance, a newly discovered species in Okinawa lives in forests and helps decompose dead wood.

　Cockroaches are also highly nutritious. They are often eaten by reptiles or amphibians. On top of this, people in various parts of the world eat cockroaches as a valuable source of
25　nutrition.

　There has long been a debate about what would happen if we eradicated bothersome insects such as cockroaches. The answer is not clear. In a predator-prey relationship, predators would simply switch to hunting other organisms if cockroaches were gone. However, understanding the full role of a single species in an ecosystem is nearly impossible.
30　There may be functions that cockroaches provide that we have not yet recognized.

Notes

intrude 侵入する / drain 排水管 / vent 通気口 / germ 病原菌 / bacteria 細菌 / shigella 赤痢菌 / salmonella サルモネラ菌 / vibrio cholerae コレラ菌 / pose（危険・問題などを）もたらす / resilience 回復力 / grease 油脂 / splatter 飛び散り / pest 害虫 / decomposer 分解者 / reptile 爬虫類 / amphibian 両生類 / bothersome insect 厄介な虫 / predator-prey relationship 捕食者と被食者の関係

▶ Comprehension

１．次の文が本文の内容と一致する場合は T を、異なる場合は F を記入しましょう。

(1) [   ] Cockroaches have been around since before humans first emerged on Earth.

(2) [   ] Cockroaches carry bacteria such as shigella, salmonella, and vibrio cholerae on
their bodies.

(3) [   ] Cockroaches can survive only by consuming human food.

２．次の質問に対する答えとして最も適切なものを (A) ～ (D) の中から選びましょう。

(1) Why are cockroaches considered a health risk?

(A) They invade homes through windows.

(B) They consume human hair.

(C) They carry harmful bacteria.

(D) They can survive on water alone.

(2) Where do cockroaches often go?

(A) To homes full of people

(B) To places full of germs

(C) To forests away from humans

(D) To places with a lot of water

(3) What role do most species of cockroaches play in forests?

(A) They are pests.

(B) They decompose dead wood.

(C) They carry diseases.

(D) They hunt other insects.

Chapter 10　What if Cockroaches Were Extinct?

Grammar Points

可算名詞と不可算名詞および冠詞の用法

① 可算名詞と不可算名詞の違い
　(a)可算名詞：2つに分けたら、そのものでなくなるもの
　　例えばpencilは2つに折ったら、もはや鉛筆ではなくなる。
　(b)不可算名詞：2つに分けても、そのものであるもの
　　例えばchalkは2つに折っても、チョークである。（だから数える意味がない）
　　※不可算名詞の例：物質名詞（meat, waterなど）、抽象概念（love, musicなど）、種々のものを集めた概念（furniture[家具]、information[情報]など）
② 可算名詞の形：a+N, the+N, N-s, the N-sの4つの形　[N-sは複数形]
③ 冠詞の注意すべき用法
　(1) 2つのものがあると、一方をone、もう一方をthe otherで示す。
　(2) 「〜につき…」は、<…a+〜>で表せる。⇒10,000 steps a day（1日1万歩）
　(3)単数の新情報は<a+〜>で導入する。
　　⇒ There is a book on the desk.（机の上に本がある。）/×There is the book …

次の英文の（　）内に入る適切な語(句)を(A)〜(D)の中から選びましょう。

(1) Humans are invading the cockroaches' territory, and not (　　　) other way around.
　(A) one　　　(B) only　　　(C) the　　　(D) that

(2) It is thought that humans lose 50 to 100 hairs (　　　) day.
　(A) a　　　(B) an　　　(C) one　　　(D) the

(3) Once invaded, we may not be able to remove all cockroaches from under the floor or in (　　　).
　(A) a furniture　(B) furniture　(C) furnitures　(D) one furniture

(4) Cockroaches are able to survive for a long time on a diet of (　　　) alone.
　(A) a water　(B) the water　(C) water　(D) waters

(5) There has long been (　　　) about what would occur if we eradicated harmful insects.
　(A) a debate　(B) debated　(C) debates　(D) that debate

69

Composition Clues

次の英文の（　　）内の語(句)を並べ替えて、日本語訳に合う英文にしましょう。

(1) Cockroaches (allow / bodies / harbor / their / to) bacteria.
ゴキブリは体内に細菌を宿すことができます。
(　　　　　　　　　　　　　　　　　　　　　　　　　　　　)

(2) Cockroaches (attempt / food / infest / sources / to) in homes.
ゴキブリは家庭内の食料源を狙って侵入を試みます。
(　　　　　　　　　　　　　　　　　　　　　　　　　　　　)

(3) Cockroach droppings are (diseases / full / of / pathogens / that cause).
ゴキブリの糞は病気を引き起こす病原体でいっぱいです。
(　　　　　　　　　　　　　　　　　　　　　　　　　　　　)

(4) Insects (are attracted / as / garbage / such / to) food crumbs.
昆虫は食べ物のかけらのようなゴミに引き寄せられます。
(　　　　　　　　　　　　　　　　　　　　　　　　　　　　)

(5) Humans should control cockroach populations, and (around / not / other / the / way).
人間はゴキブリの個体数を管理すべきであり、その逆ではありません。
(　　　　　　　　　　　　　　　　　　　　　　　　　　　　)

Chapter 10 What if Cockroaches Were Extinct?

Listening and Dictation

 1-78

次の本文の要約文を聞いて、空所に英単語を書き入れましょう。その後、その単語を下の枠内から選び、その記号で答えましょう。

Cockroaches have (1.   ) for 300 (2.   ) years. The creatures are considered a nuisance because they invade homes and (3.   ) bacteria such as shigella, salmonella, and vibrio cholerae on their bodies. Cockroaches can (4.   ) homes through drains, vents, and (5.   ) conditioning pipes. They can (6.   ) on a drop of (7.   ) for three days and consume human (8.   ) and grease, if necessary. In forests, most cockroach species play an important (9.   ) as decomposers. (10.   ) the complete eradication of cockroaches might seem beneficial, their exact role in ecosystems is not fully understood.

(a) air	(b) carry	(c) enter	(d) existed	(e) hair
(f) million	(g) role	(h) survive	(i) water	(j) while

科学よもやま話 10. 　世界最大のゴキブリ

　世界最大のゴキブリはヨロイモグラゴキブリかマダガスカルオオゴキブリと言われています。体長は7〜8cm、体重は30g程度です。想像しただけでも寒気がしますが、私たちがよく目にするゴキブリとは見栄えも動きも異なります。大きなダンゴムシといった感じでしょうか。普通のゴキブリとは異なり、ゆっくり動きます。また、飛んで向かってくるようなこともありません。見ているとだんだんかわいらしく思えてくるかもしれません。日本でもペットとして販売されており、YouTubeにも多数の動画がアップされています。

Talk and Discussion

次の2つのトピックでトークまたはディスカッションをしましょう。

1. What animal do you fear most, and why?

2. What are some animals that are hated by humans, but are beneficial to humankind?

Useful Expressions

(1) The animal I fear most is …. .
(2) The reason why … is because …. .
(3) It is often said that …. . [=We often hear that …. .]
(4) It can be explained in many ways, but I will say …. .
(5) For the foregoing three reasons, I would like to conclude …. .

コミュニケーションのコツ 10.　＜意外な意味に注意する＞

　英語は、基本的な単語ほど注意すべきでしょう。というのは、色々な意味を持っている場合があるからです。例えば、orderという単語は、次のような意味を持っています。
　　基本的な意味：順序、秩序、整理、調子、命令、注文
　　専門的な意味：勲章、(キリスト教)修道会・儀式、(生物学)目[もく]
　日本人がなじみのない意外な意味で、基本的な単語が使われる場合があります。例えば「逮捕する」で知っているarrestは、次のような意味で使われることがあります。
　　(1) The spread of the disease was arrested.（その病気の蔓延が食い止められた。）
　　(2) We were arrested by her peculiar dress.（我々は彼女の特異な衣装に目が止まった。）
　もう1つ、「『でない』と否定する」で覚えた記憶がある、denyという単語の意外な意味が分かる例文を1つ挙げておきましょう。
　　He denied her nothing.（彼は彼女に欲しいものは何でもあげた。）
denyという語は、SVO1O2の形が取れ、「O1にO2を与えない」という意味があるのです。

Animals

Chapter 11

The Mighty Tardigrade

最強の生物クマムシ

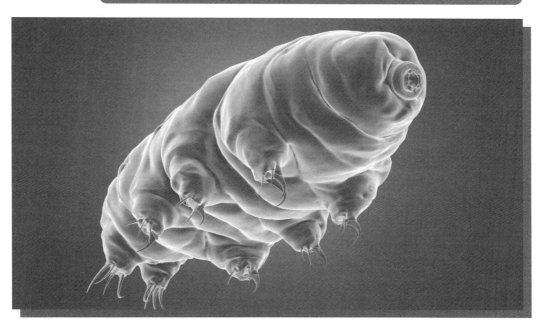

最強の生物と言われるクマムシは、海、山、熱帯のジャングルから南極まで、あらゆる場所に生息しています。このクマムシは、極度の寒冷・乾燥、更には真空の状態でも生き残る能力を秘めているようです。極小の生物であるクマムシのことをもっと知りましょう。

Vocabulary Check

1〜7の単語の意味を (a) 〜 (g) から選びましょう。

1. organism   (a) related to the body
2. physical   (b) to resist or survive
3. extreme   (c) acting against or in a contrary direction
4. lethal   (d) deadly
5. adverse   (e) to stop temporarily
6. withstand   (f) a single living plant, animal, or virus
7. pause   (g) very severe or serious

73

Reading

Tardigrades, often called water bears, are sometimes referred to as the mightiest creatures on Earth. Are these microscopic, one-millimeter-long organisms truly the toughest beings on our planet? While they might be among the weakest in terms of physical strength, in terms of resilience and survival, tardigrades are indeed the strongest.

Tardigrades can survive in extreme environments that would be lethal to most other organisms. They can endure freezing temperatures, extreme dryness, high levels of radiation, and even the vacuum of space. Most creatures would have trouble surviving even one of these adverse conditions. In one experiment, frozen tardigrades were loaded into bullets and fired from a gas gun. After being retrieved and placed in water, they remarkably revived. Tardigrades can withstand impacts at speeds up to 728 meters per second.

Why are tardigrades able to endure such harsh conditions? The secret lies in a state called cryptobiosis. When tardigrades lose water, they enter a cryptobiotic state, effectively pausing their metabolic activities. This state makes them incredibly resilient. Through cryptobiosis, they can survive temperatures from -273℃ to 100℃, a vacuum, pressures up to 75,000 atmospheres, thousands of grays (Gy) of radiation--about 1,000 times the lethal dose for humans, and exposure to outer space for ten days. There is still much left to discover about the resiliency afforded by entering a cryptobiotic state.

Despite being the most resilient creatures on Earth, tardigrades are not immortal. They can be killed by fire, rapid freezing, or being physically crushed. Their ability to withstand stress only applies when they are in a cryptobiotic state. Even in this state, they will die if subjected to enough physical pressure. Tardigrades are also challenging to keep in captivity, and their lifespan varies widely in different studies, ranging from several days to a few months, or up to a year.

However, in a cryptobiotic state, they have an extended lifespan. While there is debate about counting this state as being alive, one astonishing report mentioned that tardigrades were revived and able to reproduce after being frozen in cryptobiosis for 30 years. Additionally, tardigrades can reproduce without males, and they lack developed respiratory organs, absorbing oxygen directly through their skin. These fascinating traits indicate that as research progresses, we will likely uncover even more remarkable aspects of the tardigrade's biology.

Notes

tardigrade クマムシ / microscopic ごく小さい / radiation 放射線 / vacuum 真空 / retrieve 回収する / harsh 厳しい / cryptobiosis クリプトビオシス (「隠された生命活動」⇒動物が乾燥などの厳しい環境に対して、活動を停止する無代謝状態) / metabolic activities 代謝活動 / outer space 宇宙空間 / afford 得る / immortal 不死の / keep in captivity 飼育する / lifespan 寿命 / respiratory 呼吸器の

Chapter 11 The Mighty Tardigrade

❯ Comprehension

1．次の文が本文の内容と一致する場合は T を、異なる場合は F を記入しましょう。

(1) [　　　] Tardigrades are known for their mental strength.

(2) [　　　] Tardigrades could not survive being fired from a gas gun.

(3) [　　　] Cryptobiosis allows tardigrades to survive extreme conditions.

2．次の質問に対する答えとして最も適切なものを (A) 〜 (D) の中から選びましょう。

(1) What is cryptobiosis?

(A) A state of high metabolic activity

(B) A state where metabolic activities are paused

(C) A process of rapid growth

(D) A phase of increased reproduction

(2) Which of the following is NOT mentioned as a scenario in which tardigrades can survive?

(A) High levels of radiation

(B) Intense heat

(C) Extreme dryness

(D) The vacuum of space

(3) In which way can tardigrades certainly be killed?

(A) By pouring salt water on them

(B) By slowly freezing them

(C) By fire

(D) By throwing them

75

Grammar Points

否定辞

① unは基本的な単語（短い単語や易しい単語）に付き、inは高度な単語に付く。
　⇒ unkind、unthinkable、uneatable / intolerant, incredible, inedible
② ＜un＋動詞＞は、反対の行為を表す。
　⇒ tie（結ぶ）↔ untie / button（ボタンを掛ける）↔ unbutton
③ disは主に形容詞について「不」を表す。⇒ dishonest, dissatisfied など
④ aは「無」を表すことが多い。⇒ atheism（無神論）、apathy（無感動）など
⑤ antiは「反」を表す。⇒ anti-American（反米の）、anti-choice（中絶反対の）など
⑥ counterは「反」を表す。⇒ counterclockwise（反時計回りの）など
⑦ malは「悪」、misは「誤」を表す。⇒ malignancy（悪性）、misuse（誤用）
⑧ nonは「禁止」や「欠如」を表す。
　⇒ nonsmoking（禁煙）、non-alcoholic（アルコールが入っていない）、nonage（未成年）

次の英文の（　）内に入る適切な語（句）を (A)~(D) の中から選びましょう。

(1) After they were retrieved and (　　　) in water, the tardigrades remarkably revived.
　(A) displaced　　(B) displacing　　(C) placed　　(D) placing

(2) Tell us why tardigrades are (　　　) to put up with such severe conditions.
　(A) able　　(B) disable　　(C) inability　　(D) incapable

(3) This cryptobiotic state makes the insects (　　　) strong.
　(A) disbelieve　　(B) incredible　　(C) incredibly　　(D) unbelievable

(4) Despite the fact that tardigrades are so resilient, they are not (　　　).
　(A) immortal　　(B) immortality　　(C) mortal　　(D) mortality

(5) As research progresses, we are likely to (　　　) even more outstanding aspects of the tardigrade's biology.
　(A) cover　　(B) discovering　　(C) recover　　(D) uncover

▶ Composition Clues

次の英文の（　　）内の語(句)を並べ替えて、日本語訳に合う英文にしましょう。

(1) Tardigrades are also (as / bears / referred / to / water).
　　クマムシは「水のクマ」とも呼ばれます。
　　(　　　　　　　　　　　　　　　　　　　　　　　　　　　　　　　)

(2) Tardigrades' resilience (despite / extreme / makes / survive / them) conditions.
　　クマムシはその回復力により極限環境にもかかわらず生存することができます。
　　(　　　　　　　　　　　　　　　　　　　　　　　　　　　　　　　)

(3) They can survive (dehydration / of / ten years / to / up).
　　彼らは脱水状態で最大十年間生存することができます。
　　(　　　　　　　　　　　　　　　　　　　　　　　　　　　　　　　)

(4) Tardigrades are unmatched (ability / in / of / survival / terms).
　　クマムシは生存能力において比類のない存在です。
　　(　　　　　　　　　　　　　　　　　　　　　　　　　　　　　　　)

(5) The micro-animal's uniqueness (in / lies / size / small / their).
　　その微小動物のユニークさはその小さなサイズにあります。
　　(　　　　　　　　　　　　　　　　　　　　　　　　　　　　　　　)

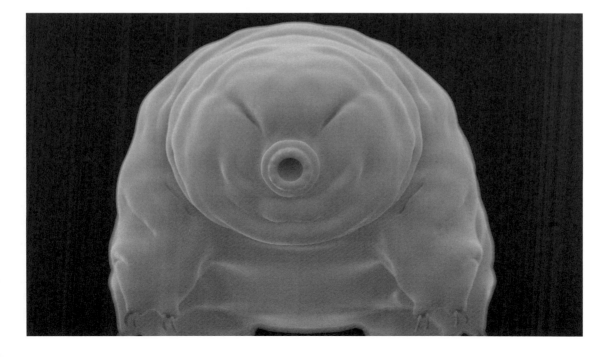

Listening and Dictation

 1-84

次の本文の要約文を聞いて、空所に英単語を書き入れましょう。その後、その単語を下の枠内から選び、その記号で答えましょう。

　　　Tardigrades, also known as water bears, are tiny organisms that can survive in (1.　　　　　) environments. They can (2.　　　　　) freezing temperatures, high (3.　　　　　) of radiation, and even the (4.　　　　　) of space. Their resilience is due to a state called cryptobiosis, where they (5.　　　　　) their metabolic activities. In this state, tardigrades can survive temperatures from -273℃ to 100℃, pressures up to 75,000 atmospheres, and (6.　　　　　) to outer space. Despite their resilience, tardigrades are not (7.　　　　　) and can be killed by fire, rapid freezing, or being physically crushed. They are also difficult to keep in (8.　　　　　), with lifespans varying widely in different studies. However, when in a cryptobiotic state, they can (9.　　　　　) for extended periods, with some reports stating that they were revived after (10.　　　　　) years in cryptobiosis.

(a) 30　　(b) captivity　　(c) endure　　(d) exposure　　(e) extreme
(f) immortal　　(g) levels　　(h) pause　　(i) survive　　(j) vacuum

科学よもやま話 11. クマムシの特殊能力を活用する

　これまで、私たち人間は生物の特長をうまく利用してきました。生物模倣*（biomimicry）は様々な分野で見ることができます。たとえばヨーグルトの蓋にヨーグルトが付着しないのは蓮の葉の表面を模倣した超撥水性の素材を使用しているからです。また、新幹線の空気抵抗を低減するための技術はフクロウとカワセミを模倣しています。クマムシは、特殊なタンパク質「Dsup」（Damage suppressor）を持っており、これがDNAを保護し、損傷を修復する能力を高めていることが発見されました。Dsupは、放射線や酸化ストレスからDNAを守る働きをしており、このタンパク質の機能は他の生物にも応用可能であると期待されています。

*バイオミメティクスとも言う。

Chapter 11　The Mighty Tardigrade

▶ Talk and Discussion

次の２つのトピックでトークまたはディスカッションをしましょう。

1. What animal do you think is the strongest in the world?
_____
_____

2. Name some of the endangered species and discuss how to protect them.
_____
_____

Useful Expressions

(1) I should say that the strongest animal is …. .

(2) I have a keen interest in that field because …. .

(3) There are a wide variety of endangered animals in the world; this time I say …. .

(4) It is important for us to do … because …. .

(5) From a biological point of view, I have to say …. .

コミュニケーションのコツ 11.　＜スピーキングの 6C ＞

その1　Correct …………… 発音や文法が正しいこと
その2　Concise …………… 文章が簡潔であること
その3　Consistent ……… 論理的につじつまが合うこと
その4　Concrete ………… 具体的な例示や説明があること
その5　Clear ……………… 言いたい内容がはっきりしていること
その6　Considerate ……… 読み手に対して思いやりがあること

6Cの基盤にはどんなことが必要なのかを以下に示す。
　　その1　Correct …………… 正しい単語と英文法の知識があること
　　その2　Concise …………… 分かりやすい文章を常に意識すること
　　その3　Consistent ……… 論理的な文章の構築の仕方を学んでいること
　　その4　Concrete ………… パラグラフやエッセイの基本構造を理解していること
　　その5　Clear ……………… 客観的な情報と主体的な意見を持っていること
　　その6　Considerate ……… 文法の応用としての文体を整える能力があること

Animals

Chapter 12
The Abundance of Life on a Savanna

サバンナに色々な動物がいるのは何故？

サバンナには実に多くの種類の動物が生息しています。草食動物とそれを狙っている肉食動物が共存し、食物連鎖がうまく機能しています。サバンナで、これらの動物が生きることができるのは、サバンナに繁茂する植物と関係があるようです。

▶ Vocabulary Check

1 〜 7 の単語の意味を (a) 〜 (g) から選びましょう。

1. abundant
2. herbivore
3. carnivore
4. prey
5. food chain
6. struggle
7. concentration

(a) an animal that eats other animals
(b) more than enough
(c) the amount of a substance contained in a certain volume of another substance
(d) the natural order of animals eating other animals
(e) an animal that eats plants
(f) to have difficulty or exert effort
(g) animals hunted as food

Savannas are grassy plains with scattered trees and shrubs usually located in tropical or subtropical regions. Savannas are known for the incredible amount of animal species that make it their home. The reason for this lies in the plant life found on savannas. When plants are abundant, the number of herbivores increases. As the population of herbivores grows, so does the number of carnivores that prey on them. In the food chain, the number of living things categorized at the lower levels must be more numerous than those at the top. In the savanna, these primary producers are grasses.

While its plant life is key to its biodiversity, not all plants can thrive under the harsh conditions of a savanna. Even the hardiest plants may struggle to survive in regions with high temperatures, dryness, low CO_2 concentrations, and nutrient-poor soils.

There are plants that can grow in the tough conditions of a savanna, specifically C4 plants. Plants are classified into C3 and C4 types based on their photosynthetic processes. The "C" stands for carbon atoms, and the number following that indicates the number of carbon atoms used in photosynthesis. C4 plants contain more carbon atoms than C3 plants, and perform photosynthesis more efficiently. Examples of C4 plants include sugarcane, maize, sorghum, and millet, all of which are fast-growing. Many weeds are also C4 plants. Farmers often struggle with weeds that grow quickly, threatening to engulf the crops.

On the other hand, examples of C3 plants include rice and wheat. These plants grow more slowly and face tough competition in areas where C4 plants thrive. The size and abundance of C4 plants may block out the sunlight that a C3 plant would otherwise receive. This in turn can cause the C3 plant to struggle to perform photosynthesis. However, C4 plants do not always have the upper hand. If they did, all plants on Earth would be C4 plants, but this is not the case.

C4 plants consume a lot of energy for photosynthesis. While they have an advantage in conditions with plenty of sunlight, high temperatures, and dryness, they are at a disadvantage in environments with less sunlight. During colder periods, C3 plants that grew earlier can block sunlight from reaching C4 plants, allowing C3 plants to dominate. Plants have been locked in fierce competition for millions of years, quietly striving for dominance to this day.

Notes

savanna サバンナ / grassy plain 草原 / scattered 散在した / shrub 低木 / subtropical region 亜熱帯地域 / biodiversity 生物多様性 / harsh condition 過酷な条件 / photosynthetic process 光合成過程 / carbon atom 炭素原子 / sugarcane サトウキビ / maize トウモロコシ / sorghum モロコシ / millet キビ / weed 雑草 / threatening 脅威となる / engulf 飲み込む / have the upper hand 優位に立つ / fierce 激しい

❯ Comprehension

１．次の文が本文の内容と一致する場合は T を、異なる場合は F を記入しましょう。

(1) [　　　] Savannas are typically found in temperate regions.

(2) [　　　] The biodiversity of a savanna is primarily due to its plant life.

(3) [　　　] C4 plants have an advantage in areas with low temperatures.

２．次の質問に対する答えとして最も適切なものを (A) 〜 (D) の中から選びましょう。

(1) What is the primary reason for the high number of animal species on a savanna?

(A) The presence of numerous trees

(B) The abundance of plant life

(C) The availability of water

(D) The high temperatures

(2) Which of the following is NOT mentioned as a characteristic of C4 plants?

(A) They grow quickly.

(B) They perform photosynthesis more efficiently than C3 plants.

(C) They thrive in nutrient-poor soils.

(D) They consume a lot of energy for photosynthesis.

(3) What happens to C3 plants when they compete with C4 plants?

(A) They grow faster.

(B) They struggle to perform photosynthesis.

(C) They dominate the environment.

(D) They force animals to eat C4 plants.

Chapter 12　Why Do So Many Kinds of Animals Live on a Savanna?

Grammar Points

助動詞

① 主な助動詞
(1) can：[1]能力（～できる）[2]可能性（～でありうる）[客観的]
(2) may：[1]許可（～してよい）[2]推量（～かもしれない）[主観的]
(3) should：[1]意見（～すべき）[2]高い可能性（～のはず）
(4) must：[1]命令（～しなければならない）[2]確信（～に違いない）
(5) will：[1]未来（～する）[2]意志（～するつもりだ）
② 助動詞の位置：主語＋助動詞＋動詞（動詞は原形）
③ 助動詞の用法で注意すべきこと
(1) 一般動詞を用いた文の疑問文や否定文を作るdo助動詞は、主語の数に一致する。
⇒ Does she study hard? / They do not play the game.
(2) ＜so＋助動詞＋主語(S)＞は「Sも～だ/する」を表す。
(3) ＜助動詞－not always＞は「いつも～とは限らない」という部分否定を表す。

次の英文の (　) 内に入る適切な語 (句) を (A)~(D) の中から選びましょう。

(1) As herbivores increase in number, so (　　　) that prey on them.
　　(A) does the population of carnivores　　(B) is the population of carnivores
　　(C) the population of carnivores does　　(D) the population of carnivores is

(2) Not every plant (　　　) flourish under the severe conditions of a savanna.
　　(A) able to　　(B) can　　(C) do not　　(D) possible

(3) An abundance of C4 plants (　　　) shut out the sunlight.
　　(A) are　　(B) may　　(C) probable　　(D) possibility

(4) We can safely say that a C4 plant limits the sunshine that a C3 plant (　　　) receive.
　　(A) does otherwise　　(B) otherwise did
　　(C) otherwise will　　(D) would otherwise

(5) It can be said that C4 plants (　　　) attain a predominant position.
　　(A) always not　　(B) always not do
　　(C) do not always　　(D) not always do

83

Composition Clues

次の英文の（　　　）内の語(句)を並べ替えて、日本語訳に合う英文にしましょう。

(1) Some plants (are / for / known / medicinal properties / their).
いくらかの植物はその薬効で知られています。
(　　　　　　　　　　　　　　　　　　　　　　　　　　　　　　　)

(2) Plants can (be / classified / families / into / several).
植物は複数の科に分類されます。
(　　　　　　　　　　　　　　　　　　　　　　　　　　　　　　　)

(3) Zebras, gnus, and gazelles, (all / are / herbivores / of / which), occupy more than 90% of animals living on a savanna.
シマウマ、ヌー、ガゼルは全て草食動物であるが、サバンナに棲む動物の9割以上を占めている。
(　　　　　　　　　　　　　　　　　　　　　　　　　　　　　　　)

(4) (hand / on / other / the / trees) provide shade and habitats for many species.
一方で、樹木は多くの種に日陰と生息地を提供します。
(　　　　　　　　　　　　　　　　　　　　　　　　　　　　　　　)
＊文頭に置かれる単語であっても小文字になっています

(5) Plants absorb sunlight (and in / for energy / it / turn / use).
植物は太陽光を吸収し、それをエネルギーとして利用します。
(　　　　　　　　　　　　　　　　　　　　　　　　　　　　　　　)

Chapter 12　Why Do So Many Kinds of Animals Live on a Savanna?

▶ Listening and Dictation

次の本文の要約文を聴いて、空所に英単語を書き入れましょう。その後、その単語を下の枠内から選び、その記号で答えましょう。

　　　Savannas are grassy (1.　　　　　) with scattered trees and (2.　　　　　) usually located in tropical or subtropical regions. The reason for the incredible (3.　　　　　) in savannas lies in the plant life found there. Abundant plants support a large number of (4.　　　　　), which in turn support many (5.　　　　　). While savannas have a high biodiversity, not all plants can thrive under the harsh conditions of high temperatures, dryness, and nutrient-(6.　　　　　) (7.　　　　　). C4 plants, such as sugarcane and maize, perform photosynthesis more efficiently and grow quickly in these conditions. C3 plants, like rice and wheat, (8.　　　　　) tough competition and may struggle to survive where C4 plants (9.　　　　　). Despite their differences, both types of plants have been locked in fierce competition for (10.　　　　　) of years.

| (a) biodiversity | (b) carnivores | (c) dominate | (d) face | (e) herbivores |
| (f) millions | (g) plains | (h) poor | (i) shrubs | (j) soils |

科学よもやま話 12.　　サバンナのプチ情報あれこれ

　サバンナの"Big 5"と言えば、ヒョウ、ライオン、バッファロー、象、サイですが、頭数のランキングではヌー、トムソンガゼル、シマウマ、水牛、インパラの順になっています。タンザニアのセレンゲティ国立公園に生息する数は以下の通りです。

1位	ヌー	1,500,000
2位	トムソンガゼル	300,000
3位	シマウマ	200,000
4位	水牛	50,000
5位	インパラ	多数生息するが数は公表されていない

　ちなみに、セレンゲティ国立公園の近くには「しりとり」で負けない地名があります。それは「ンゴロンゴロ保全地域」です。「ん」から始まる非常に珍しい地名です。

● Talk and Discussion

次の２つのトピックでトークまたはディスカッションをしましょう。

1. Can you describe any of the animals living on a savanna?

_____

_____

2. Which country in Africa would you like to visit, and why?

_____

_____

Useful Expressions

(1) From among little-known African countries, I would choose .... .

(2) If my memory is correct, I can say .... .

(3) Just to choose a couple of examples, ...

(4) The opposite is the case with .... .

(5) I cannot give a complete list, but .... .

コミュニケーションのコツ **12.** ＜WHY と HOW に慣れよ＞

日本人はYesまたはNoで答える質問には答えても、その後にWhy?と言われると戸惑ってしまうことがよくある。

Do you like dogs?（犬は好きですか）
Yes, I like them.（好きです）
Why?（何故）

この「何故」に即座に答えることができるということが、常に論理的に考えているということになる。どんなwhyの質問にも、３つぐらいの理由を考えておくとよい。
更に、whyよりも、おそらく難しい質問は、howである。

How can we possibly solve the so-called "bullying" problem?
（いわゆる「いじめ問題」はどのようにして解決可能だろうか？）

このような質問では、すぐに答えることができる人は急に少なくなるであろう。論理的思考の機会の少なさと共に、主体的な意見を持っていないことも、即座に答えることができない理由であろう。

Physics and Chemistry

Chapter 13
What Makes Stone-roasted Sweet Potatoes So Sweet

石焼き芋が甘くなる本当の理由

焼き芋は、石の上で焼くのが一番美味しいようです。だからこそ、「石焼き芋」という言葉が定着しています。では、一体どうして、石焼き芋が甘くなるのでしょうか？…これには、きちんとした理由があるようです。

▶ Vocabulary Check

1 ～ 7 の単語の意味を (a) ～ (g) から選びましょう。

1. roast   (a) a category within a species, based on some hereditary difference
2. enzyme   (b) to make something longer or larger in space or time
3. molecule   (c) to cook food in an oven or over a fire
4. primarily   (d) the smallest unit of a chemical substance that can exist independently
5. extend   (e) to improve the quality, amount, or strength of something
6. enhance   (f) firstly and mainly; for the most part
7. variety   (g) a protein that speeds up chemical reactions in living organisms

Reading

Have you ever wondered why stone-roasted sweet potatoes are so sweet? The key to their sweetness lies in an enzyme called amylase, which is found in sweet potatoes. Sweet potatoes are made up mostly of starch. Starch is composed of long chains of glucose molecules. Beta-amylase breaks these chains into smaller pieces. When two glucose molecules are linked together, they form maltose. When three or more are linked, they form oligosaccharides. The sweetness of sweet potatoes comes primarily from this maltose.

For the amylase enzyme to make the sweet potatoes sweet, two conditions must be met. First, the starch needs to be gelatinized. Second, the beta-amylase needs enough time to work on the gelatinized starch.

Gelatinization occurs when starch is heated with water. Raw starch is tightly bound, making it difficult for beta-amylase to act on it. Starch begins to gelatinize at around 65-75℃, which is also when beta-amylase starts to work. However, if the temperature exceeds 80℃, the enzyme is destroyed and stops functioning. To maximize the enzyme's activity and achieve the sweetest roasted sweet potatoes, the temperature should be maintained between 65 and 80℃ for as long as possible.

Stone-roasting sweet potatoes can maintain this temperature range for a longer time, enhancing their sweetness. When sweet potatoes are heated by stones, the heat radiates slowly from the stones through far-infrared radiation. This gradually increases the temperature. This slow heating process allows the enzymes to work over an extended period. Large sweet potatoes take longer to heat through to the center, giving the beta-amylase more time to work, resulting in a sweeter taste. Therefore, choosing a large stone-roasted sweet potato generally ensures a sweeter flavor.

This process is quite fascinating, especially when we consider why the gelatinization temperature range for starch varies. This variation is due to the climate where the sweet potatoes are grown. The same variety of sweet potatoes will have different gelatinization temperatures depending on whether they were grown in a cold or warm region. Sweet potatoes grown in colder climates have a lower gelatinization temperature. They start producing maltose at lower temperatures, allowing beta-amylase to work for a longer time and resulting in a sweeter taste. When choosing sweet potatoes, it's a good idea to consider not only the variety, but also the region where they were grown.

Notes

amylase アミラーゼ / starch でんぷん / glucose グルコース / beta-amylase ベータアミラーゼ / maltose マルトース / oligosaccharide オリゴ糖 / gelatinize 糊化する / tightly bound 強く結合している / far-infrared radiation 遠赤外線放射

Chapter 13　The Reason Why Stone-roasted Sweet Potatoes Are So Sweet

▶ Comprehension

１．次の文が本文の内容と一致する場合は T を、異なる場合は F を記入しましょう。

(1) [　　] Sweet potatoes are primarily made up of oligosaccharides.

(2) [　　] Starch begins to gelatinize at around 80℃.

(3) [　　] Sweet potatoes grown in colder climates generally have higher gelatinization temperatures.

２．次の質問に対する答えとして最も適切なものを (A) ～ (D) の中から選びましょう。

(1) What makes sweet potatoes sweet?

(A) The variety of sweet potato

(B) The presence of the beta-amylase enzyme

(C) The process of roasting

(D) The amount of starch

(2) Why is the temperature range of 65-80℃ important?

(A) It is the optimal range for beta-amylase activity.

(B) It is when the starch fully decomposes.

(C) It prevents the sweet potatoes from burning.

(D) It enhances the flavor of oligosaccharides.

(3) What is the effect of the heating process on large sweet potatoes?

(A) It makes them less sweet.

(B) It gives beta-amylase more time to work.

(C) It shortens the time for beta-amylase activity.

(D) It decreases the gelatinization temperature.

Grammar Points

ING 形（動名詞と現在分詞）

- 動名詞　名詞の役割をする。
  ① 主語・目的語・補語となる。
  ② 名詞（N）の直前において「〜のためのN」の意味を作る。
  　⇒ a sleeping car = a car for sleeping（寝台車）
- 現在分詞
  ① be＋現在分詞で「進行中」と「近未来」を表す。
  　⇒ studying（勉強中）と coming（もうすぐ来る）
  ② 形容詞用法：名詞（N）の前または後ろに置き「〜しているN」を表す。
  ③ 副詞用法（＝分詞構文）：文の前または後ろに置き「〜しながら」などを表す。

次の英文の( )内に入る適切な語(句)を (A)~(D) の中から選びましょう。

(1) The (　　　) described above makes it possible for the enzymes to work over an extended period.

　　(A) heating slow process　　　　(B) process slow heating
　　(C) slow heating process　　　　(D) slow process heating

(2) It takes a longer time for large sweet potatoes to get warm through to the center, (　　　) the beta-amylase more time to work.

　　(A) give　　　(B) given　　　(C) giving　　　(D) to give

(3) The larger the size of a sweet potato is, the sweeter flavor it (　　　) when it is stone-roasted.

　　(A) produce　　(B) produces　　(C) producing　　(D) is producing

(4) Sweet potatoes start (　　　) maltose at lower temperatures, allowing beta-amylase to work for a longer time and resulting in a sweeter taste.

　　(A) produce　　(B) produced　　(C) produces　　(D) producing

(5) (　　　) sweet potatoes, it is advisable to consider both the variety and the region where they were grown.

　　(A) What choose　　　　(B) What choosing
　　(C) When choosing　　　(D) When to choose

Chapter 13 The Reason Why Stone-roasted Sweet Potatoes Are So Sweet

> Composition Clues

次の英文の（　　）内の語(句)を並べ替えて、日本語訳に合う英文にしましょう。

(1) The clue to the sweetness of a stone-roasted sweet potato (an / called / enzyme / in / lies) amylase.
石焼き芋の甘さの鍵はアミラーゼという酵素にあります。
(　　　　　　　　　　　　　　　　　　　　　　　　　　　　)

(2) We (can / maintain / range / temperature / this) for a long period if we stone-roast sweet potatoes.
石焼き芋にすると、我々はこの温度範囲を長期間維持することができます。
(　　　　　　　　　　　　　　　　　　　　　　　　　　　　)

(3) When sweet (are / by / heated / potatoes / stones), the heat radiates slowly.
サツマイモが石によって加熱されると、熱がゆっくりと放射されます。
(　　　　　　　　　　　　　　　　　　　　　　　　　　　　)

(4) The size of a (determines / generally / its / stone-roasted / sweet potato) sweetness.
石焼き芋の大きさが、一般的に甘さの決め手となります。
(　　　　　　　　　　　　　　　　　　　　　　　　　　　　)

(5) The gelatinization temperature range for starch (climate / depending / on / the / varies).
でん粉の糊化温度範囲は気候により異なります。
(　　　　　　　　　　　　　　　　　　　　　　　　　　　　)

Listening and Dictation

次の本文の要約文を聞いて、空所に英単語を書き入れましょう。その後、その単語を下の枠内から選び、その記号で答えましょう。

There is an (1.　　　　) called amylase found in sweet potatoes that (2.　　　　) to their sweetness. Sweet potatoes are (3.　　　　) made up of starch, which is (4.　　　　) of long chains of glucose molecules. When heated with water, starch gelatinizes, allowing beta-amylase to break down the starch into smaller (5.　　　　). This process produces maltose, which makes the sweet potatoes sweet. The (6.　　　　) temperature for this reaction is between 65 and 80℃. Stone-roasting helps (7.　　　　) this temperature range for an (8.　　　　) period, allowing the beta-amylase more time to work. Sweet potatoes grown in colder (9.　　　　) have lower gelatinization temperatures, (10.　　　　) in a sweeter taste.

(a) climates　(b) composed　(c) contributes　(d) enzyme　(e) extended
(f) maintain　(g) optimal　(h) pieces　(i) primarily　(j) resulting

---

科学よもやま話 13. 「サツマイモ」の面白雑学

サツマイモは、ナス目ヒルガオ科サツマイモ属のイモですが、このヒルガオ科サツマイモ属にはアサガオも属しています。サツマイモとアサガオは同じ仲間なので、サツマイモの花はアサガオに似ています。一方、ジャガイモはサツマイモと同じナス目ですが、ナス科ナス属に属しています。

我々が食べているサツマイモは根の部分（肥大化したもの）を食用としているのに対し、ジャガイモは茎の部分（地下に伸びた茎が膨らんだもの）を食べています。

サツマイモの一種ににんじん芋というのがあり、中身が鮮やかなオレンジ色をしています。生産量が少ない貴重な品種です。

世界の約半分以上のサツマイモが中国で生産されています。2位以降7位までは、それぞれ、マラウイ、タンザニア、ナイジェリア、アンゴラ、ルワンダ、ウガンダで、アフリカが占めています。8位がインド、9位が米国で、日本は16位です（2022年）。

Chapter 13　The Reason Why Stone-roasted Sweet Potatoes Are So Sweet

▶ Talk and Discussion

次の２つのトピックでトークまたはディスカッションをしましょう。

1. When you prepare food, do you ever think about the science behind the cooking method? Why or why not?

_____
_____

2. Do you prefer roasting, grilling, or frying as a cooking method for meat, fish, vegetables, etc?

_____
_____

Useful Expressions

(1) I believe it's (not) important to consider …． .
(2) Maybe OK?
(3) OK.
(4) I think it depends (very much) on …． .
(5) To sum up my views, …． .

コミュニケーションのコツ 13.　＜柔らかなトークのコツは、譲歩表現から＞

　ディスカッション中に、いきなり、You are wrong.と言ったり、常に、I think …を用いて自分の意見のみを強調したりするのは、相手にとって気分の良いことではありません。「譲歩」がコミュニケーションの潤滑油になるものです。幾つか、参考になる例を示しましょう。

I can understand the situation, but …	：状況は理解できますが、…
There is some truth about what you say, but …	：あなたの言うことは正しいようですが、…
I feel pretty much the same way, but …	：私も全く同感ですが、…
I partly agree with your opinion, but …	：その意見にある程度同意しますが、…
This may be a bit of an exaggeration, but …	：こう言うとやや大げさかもしれませんが、…
Your idea is very interesting. However, I hope you will listen to my idea too.	
：その考えは大変興味深いですが、私の考えも聞いてくれますか？	

Physics and Chemistry

Chapter 14: Why Are Autumnal Leaves Red or Yellow?

紅葉の仕組みを科学する

秋の紅葉を楽しむ人が多いですが、紅葉の仕組みまで考える人は少ないでしょう。どうして紅葉が起こるのかを知れば、紅葉に対するイメージが変わるかもしれません。というのは、紅葉の仕組みは「会社におけるリストラ」に似ている側面があるからです。

Vocabulary Check

1〜7の単語の意味を (a) 〜 (g) から選びましょう。

1. decompose
2. complicated
3. nutrient
4. incidentally
5. sufficient
6. humidity
7. temperature

(a) Introducing a new subject related to what was just said
(b) a measure of how hot or cold a solid, liquid, or gas is
(c) the amount of water contained in the air
(d) to separate into smaller parts
(e) any substance plants and animals need to live and grow
(f) as much as is needed for a particular purpose
(g) hard to understand or deal with

Chapter 14 Why Are Autumnal Leaves Red or Yellow?

▶ Reading

Japan's autumn foliage is a spectacular sight, especially in the mountains. The vivid colors of the leaves are caused by three organic compounds known as the pigments: chlorophyll, carotenoid, and anthocyanin. Chlorophyll, carotenoid, and anthocyanin make the leaves of deciduous trees green, yellow, and red respectively. The differences in the amount of each pigment create the vibrant colors.

In winter, leaves fall to protect the tree's main body, which consists of its roots, trunk, and branches. In a way, the tree is wrapping its base in a blanket to protect itself from the cold. Trees also need energy to maintain their leaves. The weak winter sun does not provide enough energy for the tree to carry water and nutrition to its leaves, and so they fall. If leaves remained in winter, they would freeze and eventually cause the tree itself to wither.

In spring and summer, leaves contain a large amount of chlorophyll, which is needed for photosynthesis. They also contain carotenoid, which supports the function of chlorophyll. This causes the leaves to be various shades of green. To shed its leaves, a tree gradually forms an abscission layer. The sugar content produced through photosynthesis is sent to the trunk. Because of this, the chlorophyll and carotenoid decompose. The chlorophyll decomposes quicker than carotenoid, and this causes the leaves to become yellowish.

Maple leaves turning red is more complicated. The sugar nutrients of most trees are gathered in the trunk as the weather gets colder. With maples, some sugar remains in the leaves, producing anthocyanin, which causes the leaves to develop a scarlet hue. Finally, when the abscission layer is fully formed, the leaves fall.

Incidentally, besides the onset of winter, there are three other conditions that help cause the beautiful fall foliage.

First, the amount of sunshine is important. Sufficient sunshine contributes to the rate at which the leaves change color.

Secondly, humidity levels are another factor. If humidity is too low, the leaves will die before turning yellow or red.

Last but not least, the difference in temperature between day and night is important. When it is cold at night, the formation of the abscission layer proceeds smoothly. Also, a hot daytime temperature is more favorable to decomposition. Both these factors lead to the formation of beautiful autumnal leaves.

Next fall, let's enjoy the wonderful foliage while keeping in mind the magnificent and complex processes behind it!

Notes

pigment 色素 / chlorophyll クロロフィル（葉緑素）/ carotenoid カロチノイド / anthocyanin アントシアニン / deciduous tree 落葉樹 / wither 枯れる / photosynthesis 光合成 / shed（木が葉を）落とす / abscission layer 離層 / hue 色相

● Comprehension

1．次の文が本文の内容と一致する場合は T を、異なる場合は F を記入しましょう。

(1) [   ] Carotenoids are pigments that make the leaves of deciduous trees yellow.

(2) [   ] Adequate humidity does not play an important role in making leaves beautiful.

(3) [   ] When it is cold, the breakdown of chlorophylls and carotenoids accelerates.

2．次の質問に対する答えとして最も適切なものを (A) ～ (D) の中から選びましょう。

(1) What makes the leaves of a deciduous tree rich in color vividness?

(A) The coldness of winter

(B) Different amounts of the three pigments

(C) The formation of the abscission layer

(D) The amount of sunshine it receives

(2) What does a tree do to protect its roots, trunks, and branches from the cold?

(A) Begins the process of shedding its leaves

(B) Grows larger leaves

(C) Forms a protective layer around the middle of the trunk

(D) Changes the color of its leaves to green

(3) What are the three conditions that lead to beautiful autumnal leaves?

(A) Sufficient nutrition, ample humidity, and the promotion of decomposition

(B) A good amount of sunshine, enough water, and carbon dioxide

(C) Sufficient sunshine, proper humidity, and a wide range of temperatures

(D) A good amount of humidity, enough sunshine, and an abscission layer

Grammar Points

 関係詞

① 関係代名詞：接続詞と代名詞の役割をする。
  (a)人が先行詞：who（主格）、whom（目的格）、that（主格・目的格）
  (b)物が先行詞：which（主格・目的格）、that（主格・目的格）
    注1　whatは先行詞を含む関係代名詞（主格・目的格）である。
    注2　＜前置詞＋関係代名詞＞の形：直後に完全な文が来る。
② 関係副詞：接続詞と副詞の役割をする。
  (a)時が先行詞：when
  (b)場所が先行詞：where
  (c)理由(reason)が先行詞：why
  ※制限用法（コンマなし）と非制限用法（コンマ＋関係詞）
    制限用法：a book that she bought（彼女の買った本）[本を制限している]
    非制限用法：The Capital, which he bought（彼が買った『資本論』）
      注：非制限用法は、先行詞が固有名詞や限定された名詞句

次の英文の（　）内に入る適切な語（句）を (A)~(D) の中から選びましょう。

(1) There is an interesting reason (　　　) the leaves change color.
　(A) what　　　(B) when　　　(C) which　　　(D) why

(2) In winter, leaves fall because the tree tries to protect (　　　) consists of its roots, trunk, and branches.
　(A) its main body of which　　　(B) its main body, which
　(C) its main body which　　　(D) its main body, where

(3) The way (　　　) maple leaves turn red is more complicated.
　(A) how　　　(B) in which　　　(C) of　　　(D) on which

(4) Generally speaking, there are four conditions (　　　) help cause the beautiful fall foliage.
　(A) for　　　(B) that　　　(C) where　　　(D) whose

(5) A sufficient amount of sunshine will contribute to (　　　) the leaves change color.
　(A) at the rate of which　　　(B) at which rate
　(C) the rate at which　　　(D) which the rate

Composition Clues

次の英文の（　　　）内の語を並べ替えて、日本語訳に合う英文にしましょう。

(1) Let us explain (leaves / of / mechanism / the / turning) yellow or red.
葉が黄色や赤に変わるメカニズムを説明しよう。
(　　　　　　　　　　　　　　　　　　　　　　　　　　　　　　)

(2) The central part of (a / consists / of / its roots / tree) and trunk, with leaves unnecessary in winter.
木の中心的な部分は、根や幹から成っていて、葉は冬には不要になります。
(　　　　　　　　　　　　　　　　　　　　　　　　　　　　　　)

(3) In order to save energy, leaves are (fall / in / made / to / winter) by their tree, which they form an important part of in spring and summer.
省エネの視点から、葉は冬に木によって落とされるが、春や夏には木の重要な一部を形成します。
(　　　　　　　　　　　　　　　　　　　　　　　　　　　　　　)

(4) The volume and duration of sunshine contributes to (change / coloring / in / quick / the) of leaves.
日照の量と長さは、葉の色付きの変化の速度を速めることに貢献しています。
(　　　　　　　　　　　　　　　　　　　　　　　　　　　　　　)

(5) The coldness of night and the warmth of day will (both / formation / lead / the / to) of beautiful autumnal leaves.
夜の寒さと昼間の温かさの両方が美しい紅葉の形成に導きます。
(　　　　　　　　　　　　　　　　　　　　　　　　　　　　　　)

Chapter 14 Why Are Autumnal Leaves Red or Yellow?

▶ Listening and Dictation

CD 2-23

次の本文の要約文を聞いて、空所に英単語を書き入れましょう。その後、その単語を下の枠内から選び、その記号で答えましょう。

Three pigments in a (1.　　　　　　　), which are chlorophyll, carotenoid, and anthocyanin, will (2.　　　　　　) the leaf to become green, yellow, or red (3.　　　　　　). A deciduous tree chooses to shed its leaves to (4.　　　　　　) in winter. In the process of preparing to shed the leaves, chlorophyll and carotenoid are (5.　　　　　　). Because the speed of the decomposition of chlorophyll is higher than (6.　　　　　) of carotenoid, the tree's leaves (7.　　　　　　) yellow. On the other hand, during this process, some amount of nutrition (8.　　　　　) through photosynthesis may (9.　　　　　) in the leaves. Some sugar is left in the leaves, (10.　　　　　) in the formation of anthocyanin, which makes leaves look red.

(a) cause	(b) decomposed	(c) leaf	(d) produced	(e) remain
(f) respectively	(g) resulting	(h) survive	(i) that	(j) turn

科学よもやま話 14. 　　カエデとイチョウの語源は?

　カエデは秋には見事に紅葉しますが、この「カエデ」という名前の語源は、「蛙手」(カエルデ)だと言われています。確かに、カエデの葉っぱは蛙の手に似ています。「カエルデ」が訛って「カエデ」となったのは納得できます。

　一方、黄色に色づくイチョウは、その名前が、中国語の鴨脚(イアチャオ)[=アヒルの足]に由来すると言われています。確かにイチョウの葉っぱはアヒルの足の水かきに見えます。「イアチャオ」が訛って「イチョウ」になったものと考えられます。

　進化論を唱えたダーウィンは、イチョウを「生きた化石」と呼びました。植物が地球上で繁茂したのがジュラ紀(約1億5千万年前)で、そのころの植物でイチョウだけが現存し、他の植物は全て化石となっているのがその理由です。

99

▶ Talk and Discussion

次の2つのトピックでトークまたはディスカッションをしましょう。

1. Tell us about some places where you enjoyed autumnal leaves.
_____
_____

2. Where would you recommend your friend go leaf viewing?
_____
_____

Useful Expressions

(1) Let me explain …. .
(2) I recommend you (should) visit …. .
(3) I would like to tell you what I think about …. .
(4) What I want to say the most is …. .
(5) This is characterized by …. .

コミュニケーションのコツ 14.　＜テーマに沿って自由に話す＞

talk（喋る）とdiscuss（議論する）とdebate（ディベートする）には違いがあります。
・talk：特にテーマを設定せず、自由にお喋りすること
・discuss：テーマを設定して、自由に議論すること
・debate：テーマを掘り下げた論題・論点・問題点(issue)を設定して、議論すること
　※ディベートはある論題に対し、肯定側または否定側の立場に立って自分の主張をすることで、自分の立場を変えないのが原則となります。ディスカッションは、納得や感動を通じて、自らの意見を変更することも可能です。この3単語を用いて、違いが分かるフレーズを挙げてみると、talk about the trouble、discuss the problem、debate the issueとなります。トラブルを明確化し、何が問題なのかを論じるのはdiscuss、更に、具体的な論点について議論を深めるとdebateとなります。

Chapter 15: The Mystery of Water

水の不思議を考える

我々に身近な存在である水。氷になると水に浮きます。実は固体になるとその液体より重くなるのが常識です。その意味で、水は特異な物質ですが、我々は水の凄さに気付かないものです。水を基礎から学び直し、改めてそのありがたさに触れることにしましょう。

▶ Vocabulary Check

1〜7の単語の意味を (a)〜(g) から選びましょう。

1. moisture
2. highlight
3. compelling
4. aspect
5. alternatively
6. altitude
7. lowering

(a) offering or expressing another choice
(b) attracting interest in a powerful way
(c) the height of an object or point in relation to sea level
(d) a particular part or feature of something
(e) to emphasize or make something noticeable
(f) making or becoming less in amount or intensity
(g) a small amount of water in the air or on something

▶ Reading

🎧 2-24〜28

Some people lick their finger before separating papers or cash. This is due to a decrease in moisture levels in their bodies. Newborns have the highest water content, at 80% of their body weight; children have 70%; and adults have 60%. Despite this age-related decline, more than half of an elderly person's body is still water, highlighting the importance of
5　water in sustaining life.

There are quite a few compelling aspects of water. It can exist as a solid, liquid, or gas depending on its temperature. It becomes ice when the molecules are bonded and unmoving. Alternatively, it becomes a liquid when the molecules freely move while bonding and separating. Finally, it becomes a gas when the molecules vigorously move.

10　It is commonly thought that water boils and becomes a gas at 100℃, but actually it is 99.974℃. This boiling point is not constant. It changes according to atmospheric pressure. Water boils at 99.974℃ when the atmospheric pressure is 1,013.25 hectopascals (hPa). At higher altitudes, lower atmospheric pressure dramatically affects boiling. At the summit of Mt. Fuji, 3,776 meters above sea level, the pressure is about 630 hPa, and water boils at
15　around 87℃. As the pressure decreases, the boiling point also decreases, and so cooking at high altitudes and at sea level are not the same. There is also less air pressure on the upper floors of high-rise buildings. For instance, at the top of the almost 330-meter-tall Azabudai Hills skyscraper in Tokyo, the boiling point of water can be about 1℃ lower.

Freeze-drying, often found with food packaging, also uses this principle of lowering the
20　boiling point by reducing pressure. At 6.1 hPa, water boils at 0℃, but since 0℃ is also the freezing point, the water boils while remaining frozen. In other words, it sublimates from solid to gas.

There are also some other fascinating aspects of water. Water is the only substance that becomes lighter when changing from a liquid to a solid. This is why ice floats on water. The
25　opposite is the case with any other substance as solids are heavier than liquids. Interestingly, water is said to have arrived on Earth from a meteor far in the past. Also, a spoonful of water is able to store as much as one terabyte of information. Furthermore, drinking 500 ml of water before work is said to make our brains work 14% more efficiently. Water is truly a marvel.

Notes ・・

newborn 新生児 / quite a few かなりの数 / solid 固体 / liquid 液体 / gas 気体 / vigorously 激しく / atmospheric pressure 気圧 / above sea level 海抜 / principle 原理 / sublimate 昇華する / meteor 隕石 / terabyte テラバイト (TB=1,000GB)

Chapter 15　The Mystery of Water

❯ Comprehension

１．次の文が本文の内容と一致する場合は T を、異なる場合は F を記入しましょう。

(1) [　　] Newborns have the lowest water content in their bodies.

(2) [　　] Water becomes a gas exactly at 100℃.

(3) [　　] The boiling point of water changes with atmospheric pressure.

２．次の質問に対する答えとして最も適切なものを (A) ～ (D) の中から選びましょう。

(1) What happens to water molecules when water becomes ice?

　　(A) They move freely.

　　(B) They bond and do not move.

　　(C) They become a gas.

　　(D) They become steam.

(2) How does water behave at 0℃ and 6.1 hPa?

　　(A) It melts.

　　(B) It freezes.

　　(C) It boils while remaining frozen.

　　(D) It changes into a gas.

(3) Why is cooking different at high altitudes compared to sea level?

　　(A) Higher altitudes have more air pressure.

　　(B) Water boils at a lower temperature due to reduced pressure.

　　(C) Food cooks faster at high altitudes.

　　(D) There is more moisture in the air at high altitudes.

103

Grammar Points

接続詞

① 等位接続詞：語、句、文を並列させて繋ぐ。
　(a) 順接：「そして～」 ⇒ and, so
　(b) 逆接：「しかし～」 ⇒ but, yet
② 従属接続詞：文の直前に置き従属節をつくり、主文を修飾する。
　(c) 順接：「～だから」 ⇒ as, since, because
　(d) 逆接：「～だけれども」 ⇒ though, while
　(e) when ～：～するとき
　(f) while ～：～している間
　　※1　逆接的な意味を持つwhileもある（上記）。
　　※2　while ~ing の形もよく用いられる。

次の英文の (　) 内に入る適切な語を (A)~(D) の中から選びましょう。

(1) (　　　) this decline with age, over half of an old person's body is still water.
　(A) But　　　　(B) Despite　　　　(C) However　　　　(D) Though

(2) Water exists in a liquid state (　　　) the molecules are freely moving.
　(A) that　　　　(B) therefore　　　　(C) what　　　　(D) when

(3) Water is said to become a gas at 100℃, (　　　) to be more specific, it's actually 99.974℃.
　(A) but　　　　(B) however　　　　(C) lest　　　　(D) unless

(4) This means (　　　) cooking at high altitudes and at sea level are slightly different.
　(A) that　　　　(B) those　　　　(C) what　　　　(D) which

(5) At 6.1 hPa, water boils even at 0℃; interestingly, we can see the water boiling (　　　) remaining frozen, since 0℃ is also the freezing point.
　(A) during　　　　(B) that　　　　(C) what　　　　(D) while

Chapter 15　The Mystery of Water

▶ Composition Clues

次の英文の（　　）内の語（句）を並べ替えて、日本語訳に合う英文にしましょう。

(1) Water (an essential role / in / life / plays / sustaining).
　　水は生命を維持するのに重要な役割を果たします。
　　(　　　　　　　　　　　　　　　　　　　　　　　　　　　)

(2) The boiling point of water (atmospheric pressure / changes / differences / due to / in).
　　水の沸点は大気圧の違いによって変わります。
　　(　　　　　　　　　　　　　　　　　　　　　　　　　　　)

(3) Boiling (close / in / is / meaning / to) evaporation.
　　沸騰は蒸発に意味的に近い概念です。
　　(　　　　　　　　　　　　　　　　　　　　　　　　　　　)

(4) The amount of moisture in the air (and / atmospheric / depends / on / temperature) pressure.
　　空気中の水分量は温度と気圧に依存します。
　　(　　　　　　　　　　　　　　　　　　　　　　　　　　　)

(5) (evaporation / phenomenon / refers / the / to) of vaporization from the surface of a liquid.
　　蒸発は液体の表面から気化する現象のことを言います。
　　(　　　　　　　　　　　　　　　　　　　　　　　　　　　)
　　＊文頭に置かれる単語であっても小文字になっています

Listening and Dictation

次の本文の要約文を聞いて、空所に英単語を書き入れましょう。その後、その単語を下の枠内から選び、その記号で答えましょう。

Water is (1.   ) for life, making up a significant portion of the human body. It can (2.   ) as a solid, (3.   ), or gas depending on temperature. The (4.   ) point of water is 99.974℃ at standard atmospheric (5.   ), but it decreases at (6.   ) altitudes due to (7.   ) pressure. Freeze-drying uses the (8.   ) of (9.   ) the boiling point by reducing pressure, causing water to sublimate from solid to gas. Water is the only substance that becomes lighter when its liquid is changed into a solid. This is one of the (10.   ) aspects of water.

(a) amazing	(b) boiling	(c) essential	(d) exist	(e) higher
(f) liquid	(g) lowering	(h) lower	(i) pressure	(j) principle

科学よもやま話 15.　水中における音の伝わる速度

音は媒質の密度が高いほど速く伝わります。水は空気よりも密度が高いため、音は水中をより速く伝わります。具体的には、空気中での音速が約343メートル/秒であるのに対し、水中では約1482メートル/秒です。浮遊物等により多少この数字とは異なることもありますが、水分子間の距離が空気分子間よりも短いため、振動がより効率的に伝わります。音が速く伝わるのは悪いことではありませんが、注意すべきことがあります。それは、速いが故に左右の耳に伝わる音の時差がほとんどないため、音が出ている方向を認識しにくくなることです。

Chapter 15　The Mystery of Water

▶ Talk and Discussion

次の２つのトピックでトークまたはディスカッションをしましょう。

1. What are some ways water is important in our lives?

_____

_____

2. What characteristics of water do you think many people would not know about?

_____

_____

Useful Expressions

(1) Generally speaking, …. .

(2) To be more specific, …. .

(3) Let me explain how important it is for us. I will say …. .

(4) I think this is (almost) certain to be …. .

(5) I feel confident in saying that …. .

コミュニケーションのコツ 15.　＜よく似た単語の違いが分かること＞

　studyとlearn、lookとsee、talkとspeakなど似ている意味の単語のニュアンスの違いを知っておくと、正確なコミュニケーションができるようになります。これらの違いを示すような例文を挙げておきましょう。

(a) I studied German but did not learn it.（ドイツ語は勉強しましたが修得しませんでした。）

(b) I looked around but did not see anything.（辺りを見たが、何も見えませんでした。）
　もし、I listened but did not hear anythingと言えば「耳を澄ませたけれど、何も聞こえませんでした。」の意味となります。

(c) He is just talking but not speaking.（彼はベラベラ喋るだけで、ポイントがずれています。）
　もし、She is just hearing but not listening.という文を聞けば、それは「彼女はうわの空だね（＝しっかりと聞いていない）。」のような意味でしょう。

　「ヒアリング能力」の英語は、hearing abilityではなく、listening abilityです。というのは、hearing abilityが「聴力」、listening abilityが「聴解力」の意味となるからです。

107

TEXT PRODUCTION STAFF

edited by	編集
Yasutaka Sano	佐野 泰孝

cover design by	表紙デザイン
Nobuyoshi Fujino	藤野 伸芳

DTP by	DTP
ALIUS (Hiroyuki Kinouchi)	アリウス（木野内 宏行）

CD PRODUCTION STAFF

recorded by	吹き込み者
Howard Colefield (AmE)	ハワード・コールフィルド（アメリカ英語）
Karen Haedrich (AmE)	カレン・ヘドリック（アメリカ英語）

Science Alive
知って得する日常の科学

2025年1月20日　初版発行
2025年2月15日　第2刷発行

著　　者　石井 隆之
　　　　　岩田 雅彦
　　　　　Joe Ciunci

発 行 者　佐野 英一郎

発 行 所　株式会社 成美堂
　　　　　〒101-0052　東京都千代田区神田小川町3-22
　　　　　TEL 03-3291-2261　FAX 03-3293-5490
　　　　　https://www.seibido.co.jp

印 刷・製 本　三美印刷㈱

ISBN 978-4-7919-7304-0　　　　　　　　Printed in Japan

・落丁・乱丁本はお取り替えします。
・本書の無断複写は、著作権上の例外を除き著作権侵害となります。